Centerville Library
Washington-Centerville Public Library
Centerville, Ohio

DISCARD

W9-BAT-391

"Mayada's story and recipes take the reader on a delicious and intimate journey of food, traditions, and resilience. It's a book that makes you feel you are right in the kitchen with her. The delicious Syrian food will have you rushing to the store to get cooking right away! Her story reminds us how family, food, and culture can bring us together."

—Fany Gerson, chef, founder of La Newyorkina, and author of
Mexican Ice Cream: Beloved Recipes and Stories

"When we share food, we create community. Some communities and foods are inaccessible to us because we may not share a common language—*The Bread and Salt Between Us* bridges this gap effortlessly. This book connects us with a Syrian family's experience and cuisine, making the unfamiliar intimately familiar. The book does not shy away from teaching us some of the more elaborate recipes found in Syrian cuisine and, in doing so, gives us all a very meaningful seat at the table—a colorful, soulful, and inspiring table."

—Homa Dashtaki, founder of White Moustache Yogurt

"*The Bread and Salt Between Us* is a heartwarming book of captivating stories and delicious recipes that showcase the beauty of the human spirit."

—Yasmin Khan, author of *The Saffron Tales*

"Mayada and her family have a beautiful story—it began in Syria before the war and it continues here in the US. Delicious food is clearly at the center of her family's activities, and I'm grateful that Mayada is sharing her recipes. *The Bread and Salt Between Us* is a reminder, as Jennifer Sit writes, that everyday foods are a luxury that should not be taken for granted."

—Klancy Miller, author of *Cooking Solo*

"I am so happy this book exists; it's a master class of resilience, generosity, and empathy. It is an honor to have the opportunity to learn about Mayada and her family, and a joy to cook her vibrant, comforting recipes."

—Sierra Tishgart, James Beard Award–winning journalist and
former senior editor, Grub Street

"In our current political and cultural climate, it's commendable to see someone using her passion for food to step beyond boundaries. Food has always been a conduit for a deeper understanding of other cultures, and Mayada shows a picture of love and warmth through her delicious recipes."

—Jose Garces, chef and author of *The Latin Road Home*

The Bread and Salt Between Us is a powerful story of survival and reincarnation. Most importantly, the collective stories bind us all together through food and memories."

—Vikas Khanna, chef, restaurateur, and cookbook author

"Mayada Anjari's book is a beautiful testimony to the rich—and often over-looked—cultural contributions that displaced people bring to their country of adoption. More than just a collection of recipes, this book is a cultural artifact that celebrates the power of food to transcend the hardships of refugee life."

—Pierre Thiam, chef and author of *Senegal*

"In her popular dinner series, Mayada feeds people from the heart, as any good chef does. And as millions of women new to this country have done for centuries, she feeds her own family by feeding others. In the beautiful *The Bread and Salt Between Us*, Mayada's recipes tell her story of resilience and community. As you read and cook from these pages, Syria ceases being only horrific headline material, as some of its faces and lives are revealed through one family's story. Mayada's personal way of sharing food may just help change the future of our industry."

—Rebecca Charles, chef and owner of Pearl Oyster Bar NYC, Pearl Kennebunk Beach, and Spat Oyster Cellar, Maine

"I always hoped to make it to Syria, to see Palmyra and the famous souk in Aleppo, and best of all, to taste the food. Thanks to Mayada, I get to cook the legendarily delicious food myself, right at home. This book holds a beautiful and evocative story, and by buying a copy you're supporting Mayada's family and an organization committed to helping many more."

—Sara Jenkins, chef and owner of Nina June and Porsena

THE BREAD

AND SALT

BETWEEN US

بيننا خبز وملح

THE BREAD

Recipes and Stories from

AND SALT

a Syrian Refugee's Kitchen

BETWEEN US

Mayada Anjari with Jennifer Sit

Foreword by José Andrés
Photography by Liz Clayman

LAKE ISLE PRESS · NEW YORK

Text copyright © 2018 Mayada Anjari and Jennifer Sit

Photographs copyright © 2018 Liz Clayman

Photographs pages 8–9, 12, 165, 166 © 2018 Julie Goldstone

All rights reserved. No part of this book may be reproduced, stored in a retrieval system, or transmitted, in any form, or by any means, electronic or mechanical, including photocopying and recording, without prior written consent from the publisher.

Published by:

Lake Isle Press, Inc.

2095 Broadway, Suite 301

New York, NY 10023

(212) 273-0796

E-mail: info@lakeislepress.com

Distributed to the trade by National Book Network, Inc., 4501 Forbes Boulevard, Suite 200, Lanham, MD 20706, Tel: 1(800) 462-6420, www.nbnbooks.com

Library of Congress Control Number: 2018931230

ISBN-13: 978-1-891105-63-0

This book is available at special sales discounts for bulk purchases as premiums or special editions. For more information, contact the publisher at (212) 273-0796 or by e-mail: info@lakeislepress.com

Text: Mayada Anjari and Jennifer Sit

Photography: Liz Clayman

Food and Prop Styling: Mira Evnine

Book and Cover Design: Allegra Fisher

Editors: Jennifer Sit, Hiroko Kiiffner, Jeanne Hodesh

Project Manager and Production Editor: Elizabeth Gordon

Copy Editor, Proofreader, and Indexer: Suzanne Fass

Production Manager: Bill Rose

Project Director: David Mammen, Rutgers Presbyterian Church

www.breadandsaltbetweenus.org

First edition

Printed in China

10 9 8 7 6 5 4 3 2 1

For my mother and father, and for my family

CONTENTS

Foreword by José Andrés 11

Preface by Mayada Anjari 13

Introduction 21

Everyday Fare 27

Friday Night Dinners & Celebrations 76

Sweets 140

Epilogue: How You Can Help Refugees 163

Acknowledgments 167

Resources 170

Index 173

Foreword

JOSÉ ANDRÉS

Owner/Chef, ThinkFoodGroup and minibar by José Andrés

To me, food is the ultimate bridge. When we sit around the table, sharing good food and good drink, we are at our most human, our best selves. I have seen it at home in Washington, DC, when I am on the road visiting my restaurants in different cities, and when I was in Puerto Rico, working alongside the most incredible volunteers after the devastation of Hurricane Maria. As humans, we are always brought together by one thing that is both so simple and so deep: food.

Chef Mayada Anjari shows us in this book that the simple act of breaking bread together can go a long way in building community, both in the places we grow up and those we move to, out of choice or necessity. Mayada is like me—we are both immigrants. So are many, many Americans—we have more in common, more that brings us together, than we do to separate us. That is why we do not need walls, we do not need to be divided! Instead, we can gather around the table and enjoy some incredible meals together.

With this book, Mayada has added another amazing chapter to the long legacy immigrants have had on American culinary tradition. Where would American cuisine be without pizza and noodles, paella and sushi? And now we can add Syrian egg fritters (I love eggs, so I'm happy to learn a new egg dish), stuffed vegetables, and *fattoush* to our list of American traditions. Mayada's dishes are simple and delicious and perfect to cook for family—I would love to sit down with my wife and three daughters for these meals, just like her family does every Friday night.

The brilliant food philosopher Jean-Anthelme Brillat-Savarin once wrote that the destiny of each nation depends on how it feeds itself. Because of Mayada and the other new Americans like her, who have gone through so much to get here and have brought with them their stories, their cultures, their lives, I think we as Americans, old and new, have a bright destiny in front of us.

Preface

::~∻◇✕◇∻~::

MAYADA ANJARI

Translated by Dalia El-Newehy

I first learned to cook with my mother and sisters when I was young. We lived in Homs, Syria. Every Friday night, there was a big family gathering. We would wake in the morning and start cooking. My relatives would come every week. Family who lived in other cities would still come, but only occasionally. We loved to make roast chicken with potatoes, *kabsa* with chicken, and tabbouleh. Everybody got along and it was so fun to be together.

The first thing I cooked for Ahmad before we got engaged was rice pudding. Ahmad says, "The rice pudding did it!" When we married, we lived with Ahmad's parents, along with Ahmad's sister and her husband. I was friends with his sister before we got engaged. He would write letters to me and give them to his sister to bring to me. Once Ahmad and I were married and living under the same roof, his sister and I would cook together, teaching each other different recipes—fava beans, bulgur with lentils, *kofta.* Every month, we would all go to Ahmad's family's house in the country. There were beautiful olive and almond trees. We would cook the same elaborate dishes: stuffed vegetables and grape leaves, *fatayer*, desserts. Grilled kibbeh was our favorite because it fed a lot of people.

During the civil war, Homs was the first area of uprising, and it soon became clear that we could not stay. We first moved to the countryside to live at Ahmad's family's house, but after a long time with no school for the kids and no work for Ahmad, we knew we had to leave Syria. We made our way to the Jordanian border, then walked in the desert at night for hours until we were picked up by the Jordanian military. My mother and father, my brother and sister, and another three brothers who were married and had families, eventually went to live in Jordan, too. We all lived in the same town, except for one brother. It was really hard in Jordan. Ahmad was not allowed to work, but he looked for whatever jobs he could get. Once people found out you were refugees, you could be mistreated, and they were not welcoming. Money was tight and things were expensive, even the bread, so we cooked smaller meals just to get by. Each Friday my family would still get together for dinner.

When we first came to Jordan, we registered with the United Nations. We had no intention of coming to the United States, and no knowledge of the process. After a year and a half, Ahmad got a phone call. The caller asked, "Do you have family in the United States or Europe?" Ahmad answered no. Then the person introduced himself as a representative of the United Nations and asked, "Do you want to go to America?" and Ahmad said, "Of course!" The man responded, "I'll give you a call in a few days." Ahmad was so happy, but he thought someone was just kidding with him. He said to me, "Can you believe someone's playing this joke?" But then he got the second phone call a few days later. The man told him he had an interview and gave Ahmad an address in a town that was about an hour away. At first, he didn't want to go because he was sure it was a practical joke. But we talked about it and he decided to go—to find out who was pulling this prank.

After a long bus ride followed by a taxi ride, Ahmad got to the address and it was a big UN building. The security guard asked Ahmad his name, and after he was let in, he finally believed this was all true. He had his first interview, and from then until we came to the United States, it took more than one year and many rounds of interviews and medical exams for the whole family. After the second-to-last interview, we did not hear anything for seven months. We thought it was all over. Even when we finally got a call, we thought they were going to tell us it wasn't going to happen. But we had one final interview, and two weeks later, they told us we had flights and we should get ready to travel. They gave us lots of information about what to bring and what to expect during our trip and once we got to the US. They told us that members of a church in New York would help us after we arrived.

It was the first time I stepped foot on an airplane. I grabbed onto Ahmad when we took off! It was such a long trip and we were all so tired. The whole trip took about a day and a half: Jordan to Germany to the US. After we landed, it took a long time to get through immigration and customs. When we finally came out, an interpreter hired by Rutgers Presbyterian Church came up to us and greeted us in Arabic. Ahmad hugged him. We were so happy.

Others from Rutgers Church were there to greet us. Once we met them, there was a comfort in our hearts. We knew that they were good people. It was a cold, rainy night. It had been warm

and sunny when we left Jordan. The kids were in T-shirts, but people from the church had brought jackets. They took us in their cars and we drove in the night to the new apartment that they had prepared for us. It was filled with furniture, basic supplies, and even Syrian ingredients and a dinner that someone from the church had made for us. I remember it was rice with chicken and vegetables—it was really tasty. The next days and weeks were full of appointments (getting social security cards, doctors' check-ups, enrolling the kids in school), but there was always someone from the church with us, helping us with every step.

To celebrate our six-month anniversary of being in the US and to show our thanks for everything, we wanted to treat everybody to a big meal at our home. People enjoyed themselves so much that someone got the idea that I should cook a fund-raising dinner at the church. I had never cooked for so many people before—the first dinner was for seventy-five people—

and it was the first time I had ever made that much food. It gives me joy to cook the dinners and to see so many people enjoying my food. From the dinners came the idea of this cookbook.

We have been out of Syria for five years now. This cookbook and the dinners help us keep a connection to Homs. Ahmad and I came here for our children. We are thrilled that they're growing up here. We have never felt unwelcome in the US. Still, we can't help but miss our Friday night dinners in Homs, our visits to the countryside, and especially our family and friends. Now everybody is somewhere else.

When we first talked about the cookbook, I felt the same as I had about the dinners and even about the idea of coming to the United States: I was nervous, but I was excited too. In the end, I kind of knew it would all work out.

Introduction

JENNIFER SIT

Mayada had never seen a cookbook before, but she took to writing one with ease. Saturdays were for cooking and recording Mayada's recipes in her Jersey City apartment, and very quickly, a ritual developed in those weekend sessions. First, there was always piping-hot Arab coffee to sip in the living room. In fact, the first lesson Mayada shared about Syrian cooking was that to be a good cook, you had to know how to make a better-than-decent pot of coffee (if there's no foam on top, you're pretty much doomed). Coffee was accompanied by the persistent plying of snacks (fat medjool dates, Hostess cupcakes, oranges) and chitchat about the goings-on of the week. Her boys (aged twelve, nine, and eight) would invariably be either glued to a soccer match on the television or on their way out the door to the neighborhood park, soccer ball bouncing, while Jana, her two-year-old daughter, could be found alternately working herself up in a frenzy of excitement over her new guests and crashing from said frenzy.

The conversation would eventually turn to the ambitious list of dishes Mayada had planned for the day, and we would go over the ingredients, stories, and memories. With coffee cups now emptied and shopping to be done, Mayada would quietly sneak out the front door before Jana could see her leaving and get upset. We'd make our way just one block down to the C-Town—the ubiquitous New York–area grocery store—to pick up the ingredients needed for the day. (Any specialty items—bags of bulgur, bottles of pomegranate molasses, tins of ghee twice the size of a paint can—would have been purchased earlier in the week at the Middle Eastern grocery store in nearby Paterson, New Jersey.) Amid the aisles of boxed cereal, dusty bags of Goya beans, and pickle jars, we found the everyday ingredients for Mayada's recipes—a few eggplants (bigger than she was used to in Homs), some tomatoes, bunches of parsley, yogurt. Then, as our ritual would have it, while walking back to the apartment to cook, we would fight over who was carrying the most and the heaviest shopping bags, tugging at each other's bags in futile attempts to take on more. (A similar tug-of-war ensued at the end of every meal, but over who would get to wash the dishes.)

Back home, we would cook all day, with Mayada doing most of the heavy lifting, our translator gamely doing double duty with all kinds of kitchen prep work, and me scribbling in my notebook, asking questions, and recording measurements made from mismatched tea cups and a Teenage Mutant Ninja Turtles mug (which holds 1 ¼ cups, if you were wondering). Our incredible translator, Dalia El-Newehy, is an Egyptian woman with an infectious love of life and food—sussing out the differences between Syrian and similar Egyptian dishes was always a lively topic of conversation between her and Mayada (Egyptian *mulukhiyah?* Very different from the Syrian version. Way slimier, but no less adored). With Arab music playing and Jana running through the kitchen like a mini hot-pink tornado wreaking havoc, it was easy to forget that we were technically at work, especially when it came to enjoying the feast the day's labor produced. The table would practically groan with the dishes it held: tender *fatayer* pastries stuffed with spinach or cheese, smoky baba ghanouj, tiny torpedoes of beef-bulgur kibbeh simmered in yogurt sauce, crispy pita blanketed in hummus (its lily gilded with the addition of garlic sizzled in ghee), all ready to be tucked into with generous swaths of Syrian flatbread.

The cookbook took shape from those many Saturday afternoons spent together (and eventually Saturday evenings, once it was Ramadan). Mayada is not a culinary historian, nor a restaurant chef, blogger, or food personality. She is a woman who has cooked for her family, in some form, all her life—from family occasions alongside her mother and younger sisters, to trading off household cooking duties with her sister-in-law when she first got married and lived with her new in-laws, and now, as the matriarch of her own nuclear family of six. Syrian food is rich and varied, with a history that dates back to its ancient agricultural roots in the Fertile Crescent. Mayada's cooking doesn't aim to be the definitive, all-encompassing statement on Syrian cuisine. Rather, this cookbook and its recipes—humble and modest, not unlike Mayada herself—reflect the everyday rhythms of her life, the simple Syrian meals she makes for her family and friends. The dishes are unfussy and delicious, authentic to Mayada and imbued with her unwavering hospitality.

Mayada's spirit is evident not only in the more elaborate dishes (what she calls her "important dishes") that she is most excited to share—like the *mehshi* she perfectly hollows out by hand from a daunting tower of zucchini and eggplant, or the kibbeh she so deftly and expertly forms from the mound of bulgur and meat that, again, seems insurmountable. Her spirit is also in the Laughing Cow cheese wedges she swiftly wraps up in pita and whisks off to the boys while tending to multiple simmering pots, and in the still-warm *ma'amoul* cookie she hands to Jana, who, always underfoot in the kitchen, eats it with unbridled glee, huge dimples on display. Mayada's eyes twinkle with pride (always too modest to really beam) and she smiles with satisfaction, with deep dimples that are like mirrors to Jana's, when we all dig in, always eating too much, too fast, because the dishes are that good. Her spirit is there, too, in the extra scoop of *fatteh* that somehow appears on your just-cleaned plate ("Eat! Please! More!" she says) despite pleas for mercy, because another bite would surely burst you. This is the Mayada we have come to know through her cooking, and whose recipes grace the pages of this book. These are her everyday foods because the ordinary—sheer normalcy, whatever that may be—is a luxury not to be taken for granted.

Food, particularly in diaspora, is a powerful thing. It becomes a lifeline back home, a means to preserve a culture and a way of living that has been left behind. When you eat someone's food, cooked by their hand, you understand them and you experience a part of them. As the title of this book alludes, joining together to break bread forms a bond unlike any other. For many in the long history of people who have come to the United States—in positive circumstances and in tragic ones, both willingly and unwillingly—food can serve as much more than a cultural link. It can be a way to build a new life for your family and, even more, to build a future. The fund-raising dinners that Mayada cooks at Rutgers Presbyterian Church and other interfaith centers provide her with an important source of income, but also an empowering sense of confidence and independence that is vital in truly making a new place home. This book came to be as an extension of those dinners, created in the same spirit of generosity and community that made her family's journey here possible. Like the dinners, the book offers something more: an opportunity to reclaim her narrative.

On one of the first Saturdays Mayada and I met, in reference to an event Mayada was attending in the coming weeks, she asked our translator what the word "refugee" meant. She had been in the States for one year and had heard the term many times, but never knew its definition until then. Yes, Mayada's family has experienced and witnessed great tragedy—but this does not define them. Happiness, love, laughter, and joy are a part of their lives, too. Their story is not solely one of hardship but one of resilience. Mayada may have come here as a refugee, but she is also a mother, a wife, a daughter, a sister, a cook, a neighbor, and now, a friend.

A Note on the Book's Organization

This book is organized in three sections—Everyday Fare, Friday Night Dinners and Celebrations, and Sweets—that reflect the way Mayada generally approaches her cooking. There are the everyday dishes that are easy to pull together, such as mezze salads and staples like rice and quick egg dishes (meat is eaten only about once a week). If she has more time, a more elaborate, time-consuming dish might enter the fray, but those are generally for guests and extended family at Friday night dinners or celebratory occasions like birthdays or *iftar* during Ramadan (the meal that breaks the day-long fast). Mayada's family, the Abdulhamids, has a big sweet tooth, so for those extra-special meals, a homemade dessert is a must.

You won't find a lot of spices in her cooking—salt, black pepper, cayenne, and occasionally cumin or coriander. Pomegranate molasses, lemon, olive oil, ghee (clarified butter), and lots of garlic round out the rest of the staple flavors she uses. Relying on the simple ingredients to shine, the result is often greater than the sum of its parts.

Homs, where Mayada is from, is the third largest city in Syria and is located in an agriculturally and geographically attractive area in the western part of the country, very close to Lebanon. Its appealing location made it subject to conquest throughout the ages, and thus, Homsi food bears those influences, from the Ottoman Turks to the Persians. Like other cuisines of the Levant, Syrian-style meals typically consist of mixing and matching vegetable-based mezze salads, grains, and breads with heftier meat-centric main courses. In that spirit, you should feel free to pull and combine dishes from any section to create the spread that best suits your needs.

اكلات يومية
Everyday Fare

Tabbouleh

تبولة

Of the dishes prepared alongside her mother and sisters in Homs, Mayada's favorite ones were those that required the most teamwork. Whether it was *mehshi*, kibbeh, or this tabbouleh, she loved the satisfaction of taking on a task with her family. She felt that the food that hard work produced tasted all the better when you did it together. Most of the work that comes with tabbouleh is in the prep—lots of very fine chopping—and you can imagine the tower of vegetables that needed attending to when making tabbouleh for twelve. But if you use a food processor, chopping the lettuce and parsley will be much easier.

The key to a proper tabbouleh is to think of it not as a bulgur salad but as an herb salad with bulgur thrown in. It's all about the brightness of the parsley, the pops of juicy tomato and crunchy cucumber, all tossed with lemon juice and olive oil. Though she's scaled down the recipe here to make it right for a weeknight, Mayada will bulk up the salad with some lettuce, particularly for extra-large gatherings. She notes that some people like a more assertive acidic note from the lemons, so feel free to add more to your taste.

SERVES 6 TO 8

½ cup coarse bulgur

2 medium tomatoes, very finely chopped

1 cucumber, skin on, cut into small cubes

½ head green lettuce, very finely chopped (about 2 cups)

3 small bunches parsley, leaves and tender stems, finely chopped (about 4 ½ cups)

Juice of 2 lemons

⅓ cup olive oil

1 teaspoon salt

Pinch of cayenne pepper

1 Place the bulgur in a large bowl and add enough hot water to cover. Let soak for at least 10 to 15 minutes, until the bulgur is fluffy and has absorbed all the water. If it hasn't, carefully drain off the excess.

2 Add the tomatoes, cucumber, lettuce, and parsley. Gently toss to combine.

3 In a small bowl, stir together the lemon juice, olive oil, salt, and cayenne. Pour over the tabbouleh and toss to combine. Serve immediately.

Cucumber Yogurt

سلطة خيار باللبن

Whether it's Greek *tzatziki* or Indian *raita*, the refreshing trifecta of cucumber, mint, and yogurt is one that is well known and loved in many cuisines. The salad adds a cooling effect to dishes, and Mayada especially likes serving it with richer meat- or grain-based dishes such as Baked Kofta (pages 60 and 62) or Maqluba (page 112). Though Syrian food is usually served family-style, when Mayada makes cucumber yogurt, everyone at the table gets their own small bowl of it. Her kids like to mix the rice and yogurt all together, but Mayada takes alternating, separate bites of her main dish and the yogurt—one bite of rice, one bite of cucumber yogurt—so that each can be enjoyed on its own while complementing the other, the yogurt acting as a chilled, creamy palate cleanser.

The dried mint Mayada uses isn't the typical dusty bottle you find in a regular grocery store. She purchases large high-quality bags of it, where you can see the dried whole leaves and stems. The large quantities disappear fast, whether in her cooking or in piping-hot sweet mint tea. If you don't have dried mint, you can substitute 1 tablespoon chopped fresh mint for every 1 teaspoon dried mint.

Note: Mayada's preferred consistency for the cucumber yogurt is thinner, almost like a chilled soup. If you prefer a thicker end result, start with less water and slowly add it until the yogurt reaches your desired consistency.

SERVES 4 TO 6

1 pound cucumbers (about 4 large), skin on, cut into ½-inch cubes

1½ cups plain whole-milk yogurt (not Greek)

1 clove garlic, smashed into a paste with pinch of salt

1 teaspoon crushed dried mint leaves

½ teaspoon salt

2 tablespoons to ¼ cup water

In a large bowl, combine the cucumbers, yogurt, garlic paste, mint, and salt. Stir in enough water to reach the desired consistency (see Note). Chill before serving.

TIP

To make garlic paste, Mayada pounds garlic cloves with salt using a mortar and pestle until a paste forms. If you don't have a mortar, chop the garlic with the salt as finely as possible with a large knife. Turn the knife blade on its side and smash the chopped garlic. Scrape it together, then smash again. Repeat until a paste forms.

Cabbage Salad with Pomegranate Molasses

سلطة ملفوف   MALFOUF

Learning the language of a new place is a vital aspect of feeling comfortable in a community. When Mayada's family first came to the United States, they knew a little English (how to count, colors, days of the week), but not much. Bill Bailey, a volunteer from the Rutgers Presbyterian Church and a former ESL (English as a second language) teacher, has guided the family through many English lessons. He says, "From the beginning, I could see that our twice-a-week meetings would be fruitful for all of us. How could they be otherwise? They had boundless enthusiasm, appreciation, and focus, and a wonderful sense of humor that led to many uproarious moments." Sometimes, there were quizzes, which the whole family loved. "I would stress that they must work on their own—a futile request, as Mayada could not avoid looking over her shoulder at Ahmad's quiz and pointing out the answers if he was stumped," Bill recalls. There are lots of practical lessons: for Mayada, cooking- and food-related words (stove, bake, stir, boil, half a cup), and for Ahmad, words related to his job driving and parking cars (turn left, go straight, back up).

Of course, many times those lessons ended with a delicious dinner that Mayada prepared for her family and Bill. Bill's favorites were always her salads, especially this one. It is a simple, colorful cabbage salad that gets a punch of tart flavor from pomegranate molasses.

SERVES 6 TO 8

⅓ cup pomegranate molasses

Juice of ½ lemon

⅓ cup olive oil

½ teaspoon cayenne pepper

1 tablespoon salt

1½ pounds tomatoes, cut into medium cubes

4 cups coarsely chopped green cabbage (about ½ small head)

4 cups coarsely chopped red cabbage (about ½ small head)

1 In a small bowl, whisk together the pomegranate molasses, lemon juice, olive oil, cayenne, and salt.

2 Place the tomatoes and cabbages in a large bowl and toss to combine. Add just enough dressing to coat the vegetables; you may have extra. Toss again and serve immediately.

Baba Ghanouj

بابا غنوج

Baba ghanouj is a classic mezze dip in the Levant that combines mashed charred eggplant with tahini, yogurt, and garlic. Every cook has her own proportions and additions, but Mayada takes a page from the Homs specialty *batarsh*, which incorporates a greater amount of yogurt than tahini (some versions nix the tahini altogether). With less sesame, the result is a dip that's much lighter in taste and consistency. The key to baba ghanouj is charring the eggplant directly over an open flame, which gives the dish its unmistakable smoky flavor. A side of pita for scooping is a must.

SERVES 4 TO 6

2 pounds eggplant

¾ cup plain whole-milk yogurt (not Greek)

2 tablespoons tahini

1 or 2 cloves garlic, very finely chopped

Salt

Olive oil, for serving

Pinch of cayenne pepper, for serving

1 If you have a gas stove, place the eggplants directly on the burner and turn the heat to high. Cook for 15 to 20 minutes, rotating as necessary, until the eggplants are charred all over and look slightly deflated. (You can also do this under the broiler.) Transfer the eggplants to a plate to cool.

2 When the eggplants are cool enough to handle, cut in half lengthwise. Scoop out the flesh into a large bowl. Discard the charred skin and drain off any excess liquid. Mash with a pestle, wooden spoon, or fork until a rough paste forms.

3 Add the yogurt, tahini, garlic, and ½ teaspoon salt. Stir vigorously until thoroughly combined. Season with salt to taste. Transfer to a serving dish and top with a drizzle of olive oil and the cayenne.

Vegetable and Crispy Pita Salad

فتوش   **FATTOUSH**

Homs, located along the famed Orontes River and next to the Homs Gap, is surrounded by rich, fertile land. The river flows from Lebanon through Homs and Turkey, and into the Mediterranean. The Homs Gap, a pass between northern and southern mountain ranges, and the Orontes both helped establish Homs as a vibrant trading center and gateway between the Mediterranean Sea coast and Syria's mainland. Given Homs's strong agricultural roots, it is no surprise that there is an equally strong love of fresh vegetables in Mayada's home. To Mayada, a meal doesn't feel complete without some kind of a salad on the table. When she was growing up, any dish with lots of vegetables was always her father's favorite, particularly this one.

And what's not to love about a salad that gets topped with crispy fried pita? Mayada serves her *fattoush* with the pita on top so it's crunchy at first, but once she starts to eat, she mixes it in her bowl so the bread soaks up the vinaigrette (the extra water in it is for this very purpose). This recipe is Mayada's go-to mix of vegetables for the salad, but feel free to add other fresh vegetables and herbs that you love.

Note: Adding the water to the salad may seem counterintuitive, but this is Mayada's preference, as she likes the water to soak into the pita once the salad is mixed. Depending on how juicy your cucumbers and tomatoes are, you may not need it, so feel free to omit or add less.

SERVES 6 TO 8

Vegetable oil, for frying

1 large Syrian flatbread or 2 to 3 standard-size pitas, torn into 1½-inch pieces (about 3 cups)

1 pound cucumbers, skin on, cut into small cubes (about 4 cups)

1 pound tomatoes (2 medium), cut into small cubes (about 2 cups)

½ head green lettuce, such as romaine, finely chopped (about 2 cups)

½ small green bell pepper, finely chopped (about ½ cup)

2 tablespoons finely chopped white onion

Juice of 1 lemon

2 tablespoons olive oil

½ teaspoon salt

½ teaspoon crushed dried mint leaves

Pinch of cayenne pepper

¼ cup water (optional; see Note)

¾ cup chopped parsley, leaves and tender stems (about ½ small bunch)

1   Line a large plate with paper towels. Heat 2 inches of vegetable oil in a large pot on medium-high until hot. Add the pita and fry for 2 to 3 minutes, flipping the pieces occasionally, until golden brown. Use a slotted spoon to transfer to the paper towels to drain.

2   In a large bowl, combine the cucumbers, tomatoes, lettuce, green pepper, and onion. Add the lemon juice, olive oil, salt, mint, cayenne, and water (if using). Toss to combine. Add the parsley and toss again.

3   Divide the salad between serving bowls and top with the fried pita. Mix together in the bowl before eating.

Eggplant Stew

كواج   **KAWAJ**

Mayada's internal clock is uncannily on point. When making this dish, she covers the pot, layers of eggplant, potatoes, and tomatoes within, and says that in fifteen minutes it will be ready to be stirred together. The staggered cooking times and layering are key, as the vegetables cook at different rates, depending on how close they are to the hottest part of the pot (the bottom). Exactly fifteen minutes later, not one minute too soon, and without a single glance at a clock, she returns to the pot to give it that stir. She covers the pot again and says she'll check it after another ten minutes. We sit and become immersed in talking about the best beaches for the family to visit along the Jersey shore, and sure enough, precisely ten minutes go by, and Mayada rises to tend to the stew. When this impressive talent is pointed out to her, she merely shrugs with a smile and says that she just feels the time and knows because she's made this dish so often. Indeed, *kawaj* is a particular favorite meal of Ahmad's (and of her father's, too) and she often prepares it twice a week.

This comforting vegetable stew is hearty as is, but to make it even more substantial, add ½ pound ground beef, browning it with the onion before layering the vegetables, or serve with a side of Syrian flatbread.

SERVES 6 TO 8

½ cup vegetable oil

1 small onion, coarsely grated

2 ½ pounds russet potatoes, peeled and cut into 1-inch pieces

2 large globe eggplants (about 2 pounds), peeled and cut into 1½-inch pieces

1 teaspoon sweet paprika

1 teaspoon black pepper

3 teaspoons salt

½ cup coarsely chopped parsley, leaves and tender stems (a little less than ½ small bunch)

3 medium tomatoes (about 1½ pounds), peeled and coarsely chopped

Parsley leaves, for garnish (optional)

1   Heat the oil in a large pot on medium-high. Add the onion and cook for 1 minute, until fragrant. Place the potatoes on top, followed by the eggplant. Do not stir. Sprinkle with the paprika, pepper, and 2 teaspoons of the salt, then the chopped parsley. Do not stir. Cover and cook for 5 minutes.

2   Place the tomatoes on top and sprinkle with the remaining 1 teaspoon salt. Do not stir. Cover and cook for 5 minutes more, until the tomatoes begin to soften.

3   Stir all the vegetables together, cover, and cook for 15 minutes, until slightly softened. Give everything a good stir, cover again, and cook for 15 to 20 minutes more, until the vegetables are tender, the tomatoes have broken down, and the sauce has thickened. Top with parsley (if using) and serve immediately.

Stewed Green Beans, Tomatoes, and Garlic

فاصوليا خضراء مع الطماطم و الثوم GREEN FASSOULIA

In Mayada's kitchen, there are two types of *fassoulia*, both equally delicious. She makes the white bean version (page 139) mostly for special occasions, as it requires the beans to languidly simmer alongside pieces of meat. This version, with fresh green beans lightly braised with tomatoes and tons of garlic, is her everyday staple *fassoulia*. Loving garlic is a must to appreciate this recipe. First, half a head of garlic is smashed to a paste and cooked in oil, slowly melting into the background. Second, cloves from a full head of garlic are cut in half and braised, mingling with the beans and turning soft and sweet by the time they hit your plate. Serve with Rice Pilaf with Vermicelli (page 70) to soak up all the garlicky sauce.

SERVES 4 TO 6

1½ pounds green beans, trimmed

½ cup vegetable oil

5 cloves garlic, smashed into a paste with 1 teaspoon salt

8 cloves garlic, halved crosswise

½ teaspoon cayenne pepper

1½ pounds tomatoes, cut into medium cubes

1 teaspoon salt

1   Cut the green beans in half lengthwise, then crosswise into 1½-inch pieces. Heat the oil in a large heavy pot on medium-high. Add the garlic paste and cook for 30 to 60 seconds, until it softens but doesn't brown. Add the green beans, garlic clove halves, and cayenne. Stir to thoroughly coat everything in the oil and garlic paste. Add ½ cup water and stir to combine. Cover and cook for 10 minutes, until the beans are bright green. Reduce the heat to medium-low, cover again, and cook for 5 to 7 minutes more, until the beans begin to soften.

2   Place the tomatoes on top of the green beans; do not stir. Sprinkle with the salt. Cover again and cook for 20 to 25 minutes, until the green beans are tender.

3   Stir the tomatoes into the beans. Cover and cook for 20 minutes, until the tomatoes are partially broken down. Serve immediately.

Baked Pasta with Meat Sauce

معكرونة بالفرن   MA'CCARONA

In January 2017 the Khojas, the second family that the Rutgers Presbyterian Church's Refugee Task Force cosponsored, received devastating news. It had been three years since they fled Aleppo and one year since they were fully vetted by numerous agencies. Waiting in Turkey with their bags packed, ready to fly to New York in only three days' time, the family was told that due to President Trump's executive order banning Syrian refugees, their flights had been canceled. After a harrowing week ("It was a lot of touch and go. More touch than go," said Dave Mammen, the church's director of administration, programs, and special projects), a federal judge issued a temporary stay of the ban, and the family was allowed to continue their travels as planned.

When the Khoja family arrived at John F. Kennedy International Airport, a group of forty people—members of the Rutgers Refugee Task Force and other supporters in the community—was there to enthusiastically greet them. The Khojas were driven to their new apartment in New Jersey, the lease secured by the church. Just as it was with Mayada's family's arrival, the apartment was completely furnished and the closets were full of clothes, all through donations. Of course, the refrigerator was stocked with food prepared by Mayada herself. After a long and stressful journey, it was this *ma'ccarona*, along with *kabsa*, rice, and salad, that was waiting for the Khojas in their new American home. Though seemingly Italian, this baked pasta dish is a hometown favorite for many Syrians. Her family loves it— she makes it about twice a week—and she hoped that the Khojas would find it comforting, too.

In Arabic, all pastas, regardless of shape or type, are referred to as "macaroni" or "spaghetti," and indeed, feel free to use ziti, penne, or spaghetti interchangeably in this recipe.

SERVES 4 TO 6

1 pound ziti, penne, or spaghetti

¼ cup olive oil

1 small onion, finely chopped

½ pound ground beef (80% lean)

1 teaspoon salt

1 teaspoon black pepper

One 6-ounce can tomato paste (¾ cup)

1   Preheat the oven to 425°F. Bring a large pot of salted water to a boil. Add the pasta and cook according to the package directions until al dente. Drain well.

2   Heat the oil in a large saucepan on medium-high. Add the onion and cook for 5 to 7 minutes, until softened and just starting to brown. Add the beef, salt, and pepper. Cook for 5 to 7 minutes, breaking up the beef as it cooks, until lightly browned. Stir in the tomato paste and cook for 2 to 3 minutes, until dark red and well combined. Add 1 cup hot water and stir until well combined and slightly thickened. Add the cooked pasta and stir until well coated.

3   Transfer to a 9-by-13-inch baking dish. Bake for 20 to 25 minutes, until the top of the pasta is lightly browned and crispy around the edges. Serve warm.

Kids Rule

On a typical day in Mayada's home, the main objective is to keep the family happy and fed, so it may not be so surprising that when it comes to her cooking, particularly in the rush of the week: the kids rule. Mayada, like many parents, adjusts her recipes to her kids' preferences, but the food is delicious nevertheless. When asked why some dishes are especially important to her or why she cooks something in a specific way or with a specific ingredient, the answer most often was that her kids love it.

Mayada and Ahmad's three sons are kind, sweet boys who are full of laughter (Hayan, twelve; Mohamed, nine; Abdul, eight). They love soccer, their favorite subject at school is science, and they're learning Spanish along with English. When Mayada is busy cooking and Jana inevitably upturns a bag of pastel almond candies all over the floor, it is Mohamed who, without Mayada even asking, crouches down to clean them up. And when, minutes later, Jana does it all over again and the candies scatter, it is again Mohamed who wordlessly appears to lend a hand.

Mayada's boys love chicken drumsticks, pasta with meat sauce (*ma'ccarona*), and anything that resembles stuffed bread (*marina, fatayer*, pita sandwiches)—a diet that's probably familiar to many parents, Syrian or not. It took some time for the boys to adjust to the food at their school in Jersey City, but they've started to like it—especially the pizza. Mayada says, laughing, "There are a couple of things they don't like to eat at school. Mohamed would come home and try to describe this food, but he didn't know the name. It was broccoli! They do not like broccoli. We don't have broccoli back in Syria."

Scrambled Eggs and Tomato

جظ مظ   JUZ MUZ

Fun to say ("juhz-muhz") and a cinch to prepare, *juz muz* is a dish that Mayada turns to when she needs something quick and comforting. "*Juz muz* is an 'anytime dish.' If you're hungry and you need food, you make *juz muz*. It's so easy to prepare—even kids and bachelors can cook it. It's one of the first things you learn how to make," she says. Chopped onions are cooked until soft and sweet before eggs and tomato join the mix—it's as simple as that. For a bigger spread, while waiting for other dishes to cook and finish, it's easy to throw together *juz muz* as another addition to the meal (for Mayada, most likely a table already crowded with delicious foods).

A love for similar tomato-and-egg dishes can be found across the Middle East and North Africa, from Turkish *menemen* to Yemeni *shakshuka*. Different versions abound, each with its own unique touches and additions that find their way into the skillet: garlic, green chiles or bell peppers, spices such as turmeric, cumin, Aleppo pepper, and allspice, or handfuls of chopped fresh cilantro or parsley. For North African and Israeli *shakshuka*, the eggs stay whole, nestled in a rich tomato sauce and poached until just set.

Mayada prefers peeling her tomatoes so the dish cooks even faster—plus her kids, especially Jana, like to snack on the peels. Serve your *juz muz* as is, or even better, with a side of bread.

SERVES 4

3 tablespoons vegetable oil

1 small onion, chopped

5 large eggs, beaten

Salt

¼ teaspoon cayenne pepper

1¾ pounds tomatoes, peeled, cored, and cut into medium cubes

1   Heat the oil in a large skillet on medium-high. Add the onion, cover, and cook for 7 to 9 minutes, until browned around the edges and softened.

2   Add the eggs and gently stir for 30 seconds to 1 minute, until soft curds just begin to form. Stir in ¼ teaspoon salt and half of the cayenne. Continue to cook for 30 seconds to 1 minute more, stirring occasionally, until the eggs are almost set.

3   Stir in the tomatoes and season with another ¼ teaspoon salt and rest of the cayenne. Cover and cook for 10 minutes, until the tomatoes have softened. Uncover and reduce the heat to medium. Cook for 6 to 8 minutes more, stirring occasionally, until some of the liquid has evaporated. Season with salt to taste and serve.

Egg Fritters

عجة A'JJA

Though many people shy away from frying at home, for Mayada, frying was the easiest skill to learn in the kitchen. In fact, it was how she first learned about cooking from her mother, frying French fries and eggplant. And someday, when she teaches her boys to cook, it will be the first lesson they learn, too. These warm, eggy fritters will certainly be on the docket, as they're one of Hayan and Abdul's favorites. Mayada always prepares extra so she has leftovers for the week, and suggests you do the same.

SERVES 4 TO 6

¾ pound plum tomatoes, peeled and cut into very small cubes

1½ cups finely chopped parsley, leaves and tender stems (about 1 bunch)

½ small onion, finely chopped

5 large eggs

3 cups all-purpose flour

1 cup water

2 teaspoons salt

¼ teaspoon cayenne pepper

Vegetable oil, for frying

1   In a bowl, mix together the tomatoes, parsley, and onion.

2   Beat the eggs in a separate large bowl. Add the flour and water and whisk until smooth. Add the tomato mixture, salt, and cayenne. Stir until thoroughly combined; the mixture will be thick and chunky. Let stand for 15 to 20 minutes.

3   Line a large plate with paper towels. Heat 1½ inches of oil in a large heavy pot or skillet with high sides on high until hot (when you add a drop of batter, it will bubble immediately). Give the batter a good stir. Being careful not to overcrowd the pot, use a large spoon to add a few heaping spoonfuls of batter to the oil. Fry for 2 to 4 minutes total, flipping the fritters occasionally, until dark golden brown on both sides. Transfer to the paper towels to drain. Repeat with the remaining batter. Let cool slightly before serving. Store any leftovers in an airtight container in the refrigerator for up to 1 week.

Pan-Seared Coriander Chicken

شيش طاووق SHISH TAWOOK

Shish tawook is another fast, delicious dish in Mayada's repertoire that her kids love. She serves it as an easy addition to special occasion meals already full of more time-consuming dishes, or the way her kids love it best: stuffed into Syrian flatbread with sliced tomatoes and lettuce. When the season calls for a barbecue, she marinates the chicken in the spices and garlic, skewers it (*shish* means "skewer" in Arabic), and throws it on the grill, just as the popular kebab restaurants would do in Homs.

SERVES 4 TO 6

3 tablespoons olive oil

6 large cloves garlic, smashed into a paste with ½ teaspoon salt

1½ pounds skinless, boneless chicken breast, cut into ¾-inch pieces

¼ teaspoon cayenne pepper

1 tablespoon ground coriander

¼ teaspoon salt

Syrian flatbread, lettuce, and sliced tomatoes, for serving

1 Heat the oil in a large skillet on medium. Add the garlic paste and cook, stirring frequently, until softened, about 30 seconds.

2 Increase the heat to medium-high. Add the chicken and sprinkle with the cayenne, coriander, and salt. Stir until thoroughly coated. Cover and cook for 10 to 12 minutes, stirring occasionally, until lightly browned. Uncover and cook a few minutes more, stirring occasionally, until any liquid has thickened and the chicken is cooked through. Serve immediately, stuffed in the bread with the lettuce and sliced tomatoes.

Lamb-Stuffed Pitas

مارينا   MARINA

Every morning in Homs, Mayada would walk to her favorite bread bakery in her neighborhood. She'd buy the hot, fresh bread right out of the oven and bring it home for her family. With Middle Eastern grocery stores in nearby towns in New Jersey, she can find all the ingredients she needs, but the absent neighborhood bakery is perhaps the biggest change to her daily cooking routine.

Thin and pliable, Syrian flatbread is used as a utensil to neatly scoop up food with your hand, as a wrap to enclose grilled meats or falafel for sandwiches, or in this case, as the crispy exterior to a handy snack that's lightly charred on the outside and filled with spiced lamb. Similar to Lebanese *arayes* or Egyptian *hawawshi*, these stuffed pitas are simple to pull together and a delicious crowd-pleaser. During Ramadan, these disappear very quickly from the table, her kids devouring them on sight.

Syrian flatbread is much thinner and wider than the thick pita pockets you'll commonly find in grocery stores. If you can find the thinner variety, you'll fold the flatbread over the mixture into a half-moon shape. With the thicker pita pictured here, you'll stuff the pockets with the lamb.

Note: If you don't have a grill pan, use a cast-iron skillet or a heavy frying pan.

(recipe continues on next page)

Lamb-Stuffed Pitas

MAKES 10 STUFFED PITAS

Vegetable oil

1 small onion, coarsely grated

1 green bell pepper, coarsely grated

1½ pounds ground lamb

1 teaspoon salt

¼ teaspoon cayenne pepper

1 teaspoon black pepper

1 teaspoon pomegranate molasses

¾ pound tomatoes (1 large tomato), cut into small pieces

1 cup coarsely chopped parsley, leaves and tender stems (about ⅔ small bunch)

10 pitas with pockets, cut in half, or large, thin Syrian flatbreads

1   Heat 3 tablespoons vegetable oil in a large pot on medium-high until hot. Add the onion and cook for 1 to 2 minutes, until softened. Add the green pepper and cook another 2 to 3 minutes, until softened.

2   Add the lamb, salt, cayenne, and black pepper and stir to combine. Stir in the pomegranate molasses. Reduce the heat to medium. Cover and cook for 8 to 10 minutes, until browned and cooked through; frequently stir the lamb and break it up with a wooden spoon to create a fine texture. Remove from the heat and stir in the tomatoes and parsley.

3   If using pitas with pockets, split them open and stuff with the lamb mixture. If using Syrian flatbread, spread ⅓ cup of the mixture onto half and fold over the other half to enclose the filling. Repeat with the remaining lamb and pitas.

4   Heat a large, dry grill pan on high. Working in batches, brush both sides of each stuffed pita with vegetable oil and place in the pan. Cook until browned on both sides, 2 to 3 minutes per side. Transfer to a serving platter and repeat with the remaining pitas. Serve immediately.

Baked Kofta with Pomegranate and Tahini

كفتة بالفرن مع دبس الرمان والطحينة

Mayada simply calls this dish "meat in a pan," but the name doesn't quite do it justice. Kofta, a dish made with ground meat (lamb, beef, or chicken), spices, herbs, and onion, is most often shaped into balls or formed around a skewer before it is grilled or cooked in a searing-hot pan. In Mayada's version, she first spreads the meat in a baking dish, then scores the top before it goes into the oven to cook almost all the way through. A quick sauce of tahini and pomegranate molasses gets poured over the top, where it settles into all of the meat's nooks and crannies. Back in the oven it goes for the meat to meld with all the nutty, tart, and slightly sweet flavors of the sauce.

Eat this as the Abdulhamids do: with sizable pieces of Syrian flatbread you hold in your hand and use to break off hunks of kofta. Cucumber Yogurt (page 31) on the side is a must.

SERVES 6

KOFTA

2 pounds ground beef (80% lean)

½ small onion, chopped

1 cup chopped parsley, leaves and tender stems (about ⅔ small bunch)

¼ cup vegetable oil

1 tablespoon water

1 tablespoon salt

2 teaspoons black pepper

POMEGRANATE-TAHINI SAUCE

3 tablespoons pomegranate molasses

3 tablespoons tahini

⅓ cup water

1   Preheat the oven to 400°F.

2   Make the kofta: In a large bowl, combine the beef, onion, parsley, 2 tablespoons of the oil, the water, salt, and pepper. Wet your hands and mix together until thoroughly combined. Transfer to a 9-by-13-inch baking dish. Evenly spread and flatten the meat in the dish. Use your finger to score the meat, making 3 lines lengthwise and 8 lines crosswise. Drizzle with the remaining 2 tablespoons oil. Bake for 18 to 20 minutes.

3   While the kofta bakes, make the sauce: In a small bowl, stir together the pomegranate molasses, tahini, and water.

4   Remove the kofta from the oven and use a spoon to break up the meat along the score lines. Drain off some of the excess liquid. Spread the sauce over the top of the kofta. Return to the oven and bake for 10 to 15 minutes more, until browned and bubbling on top. Let cool slightly, allowing the juices to redistribute, before serving.

Baked Kofta with Tomatoes

صينية كفتة بالبندورة

It is easy to see why Mayada's "meat in a pan" dishes are such family favorites. They're simple to prepare, requiring just one pan and very little fuss. Instead of using the Pomegranate-Tahini Sauce (pages 60–61), Mayada tops this version with grated fresh tomatoes that soften and break down as the dish cooks. The tomatoes impart even more moisture to the juicy meat below, which gets divvied up at the table and, of course, eaten by hand with lots of Syrian flatbread.

SERVES 4 TO 6

1½ pounds ground beef (80% lean)

1 small onion, grated

1½ cups coarsely chopped parsley, leaves and tender stems (1 small bunch)

½ cup olive oil

½ cup water

2 teaspoons salt

1 teaspoon black pepper

1 teaspoon sweet paprika

2 medium-large tomatoes (about 1¼ pounds), halved and coarsely grated, skin discarded

1 Preheat the oven to 400°F.

2 Make the kofta: In a large bowl, combine the beef, onion, parsley, ¼ cup of the olive oil, ¼ cup of the water, 1½ teaspoons of the salt, the pepper, and the paprika. Wet your hands and mix together until thoroughly combined. Transfer to a 9-by-13-inch baking dish. Evenly spread and flatten the meat in the dish. Use your finger to score lines on top of the meat, about 2 inches apart, both lengthwise and crosswise. Drizzle the top with the remaining ¼ cup water and ¼ cup olive oil. Bake for 15 minutes.

3 Season the tomatoes with the remaining ½ teaspoon salt. Remove the kofta from the oven and spread the tomatoes evenly over the top. Return to the oven and bake for 20 to 25 minutes, until the tomatoes have broken down and lightly browned on top. Let cool slightly, allowing the juices to redistribute, before serving.

Lamb with Bulgur and Rice

لحم الخروف مع البرغل والأرز

Boil, grate, chop, slice, peel, bake, fry, simmer. Baking dish, peeler, pan, tongs, whisk, spatula, rolling pin. On the first day of cooking together for this book, sitting on Mayada's kitchen table was a notebook full of long lists of cooking words in both English and Arabic that she'd been practicing. They say one of the best ways to learn a new language is to put it into action, and Mayada got to do just that with the extra comfort of doing so in an arena she knows well: the kitchen. The language of food and cooking feels universal: how much, how long, how hot—no matter the locale or the dish, these elements are ever-present. With that dialogue easy to grasp, opening up about the life that is lived *around* the food—the memories, stories, jokes—was made all the easier.

Over the many weeks Mayada worked on this cookbook, her English improved markedly, and she delighted in using colloquial phrases like, "One for you! One for me!" One of the toughest words to master? The staple ingredient bulgur, which in Arabic is called *burghul*. Bulgur. Burghul. With only a switch of two consonant sounds, the seemingly simple word became a tongue-twister to conquer.

Bulgur—wheat that has been steamed, dried, and crushed—is common throughout the Middle East, but Mayada says within Syria, Homs is especially known for its love for and ubiquitous use of the ingredient. This is a simple, homey dish that Mayada explains is similar to what is served at traditional weddings in Syria, where it takes on a much larger scale, with generous haunches of lamb cooked for the occasion. The key to the recipe's deep flavor is cooking the bulgur and rice in the lamb broth (the butter also doesn't hurt), turning the staple grains into a rich, delicious base for the lamb.

(recipe continues on next page)

SERVES 6 TO 8

LAMB

¼ cup vegetable oil

2 pounds boneless lamb shoulder, cut into 2-inch pieces

½ small onion, thinly sliced

1 teaspoon black pepper

1 teaspoon salt

BULGUR AND RICE

½ cup medium-grain white rice

4 tablespoons (½ stick) unsalted butter

½ cup vegetable oil

2 cups coarse bulgur

2 teaspoons salt

1 teaspoon black pepper

Cucumber Yogurt (page 31), for serving

1   Make the lamb: Heat the oil in a large pot on medium-high until hot. Working in batches, add the lamb in a single layer and cook until browned on all sides, about 25 minutes total. As each batch is done, transfer it to a bowl.

2   Return all the meat to the pot along with any juices that have accumulated, and add enough hot water to cover by 2 inches. Cover and bring to a boil on high. Reduce the heat to medium-high. Add the onion, pepper, and salt. Cover and simmer for 20 minutes, until the lamb is tender.

3   Reduce the heat to medium and simmer for 10 minutes more, until the lamb is spoon-tender. With a slotted spoon, transfer the lamb from the broth to a bowl; reserve the broth separately. Cover and set the lamb aside in a warm place.

4   While the lamb is cooking, place the rice in a small bowl and add just enough warm water to cover. Soak for 10 minutes, rinse, and drain thoroughly.

5   Make the bulgur and rice: Heat the butter and oil in a large pot on medium until the butter is melted. Add the bulgur and rice and stir to coat them. Add the salt and pepper. Cook for 1 to 2 minutes, stirring frequently, until fragrant. Add 4 cups of the lamb broth (if you don't have enough, supplement it with hot water). Cover and bring to a boil on high. Reduce the heat to medium-low and cook, covered, for 25 to 30 minutes, until the bulgur and rice are cooked through and fluffy. Gently stir together to fluff.

6   Transfer the bulgur and rice to a serving platter. Arrange the lamb on top. Serve with the Cucumber Yogurt on the side.

Chicken and Potato Soup

شوربة البطاطا بالدجاج

So many of Mayada's dishes start simply with chicken in a pot. In recipes such as Mulukhiyah (page 116) and Maqluba (page 112), chicken pieces are first simmered with a few aromatics and spices (onion, bay leaves, and cardamom). The flavorful broth and tender meat are then incorporated into the dish: the liquid cooks the grains or is used as the base of a stew, and the meat becomes an accent or centerpiece. This traditional *shorba* (soup)—a favorite in her family, loved by Mayada's father—takes that familiar beginning and turns it into a nourishing dish with the addition of potatoes.

Mayada advises that you can use any chicken part, as long as it includes the bones (if using chicken breast, cut into smaller pieces before serving); she prefers removing the skin to make her soup less greasy. She says a particularly Syrian way of enjoying this soup would be to add a scoop of Bulgur Pilaf with Vermicelli (page 73) to each bowl, making it even more filling. Although Mayada serves the soup with the chicken left on the bone, feel free to remove the bones and shred the chicken meat before adding it back to the broth and serving.

SERVES 4 TO 6

2 pounds skinless, bone-in chicken thighs

¼ small onion, thinly sliced

3 dried bay leaves

3 cardamom pods, crushed open

2 ½ pounds russet potatoes, peeled and cut into large cubes

3 tablespoons unsalted butter

2 teaspoons salt

1 teaspoon black pepper

Chopped parsley, for garnish (optional)

1 Place the chicken, onion, bay leaves, and cardamom in a large pot. Add enough cold water to cover the chicken by 2 inches. Bring to a boil on high, then reduce the heat to medium. Simmer, covered, for 30 minutes, until the chicken is cooked through and tender. Remove and discard the bay leaves and cardamom pods.

2 While the chicken is simmering, rinse the potatoes under cold water and drain. In a pot over medium-high heat, melt the butter. Add the potatoes and stir to coat. Cover and cook for 5 to 7 minutes, until the potatoes begin to turn translucent. Add the potatoes to the pot with the chicken. Pour 1 cup water into the empty pot, stir so it picks up any butter left behind, then add to the chicken.

3 Add the salt and pepper. Cover and simmer on medium for 25 to 30 minutes, until the potatoes are cooked through. Serve immediately, topped with the parsley (if using).

Rice Pilaf with Vermicelli

أرز بالشعيرية

Mayada learned to cook in earnest at about seventeen years old, when she became engaged to Ahmad. Learning how to fry—eggplant, French fries—was the starting point of her culinary education, and next came one of the most important skills: how to prepare perfectly cooked rice. From there, more elaborate dishes like *mehshi* and kibbeh came, of course, but rice was a necessary foundation to be mastered as it serves as such a familiar, loved staple.

This fluffy rice threaded with thin strands of pasta is an everyday preparation that graces many Middle Eastern tables, and a few key details from Mayada make it perfect. To prevent the cooked rice from sticking together, the raw grains are first rinsed several times to remove excess starch. Toasting the rice grains then sets the exterior, which helps prevent them from clumping together once cooked. The broken pieces of vermicelli are also toasted until "red" to bring out their nutty taste.

SERVES 10 TO 12

5 cups (about 2 pounds) medium-grain white rice

¼ cup olive oil

¼ cup vegetable oil

2 cups crumbled wheat vermicelli or fideos (1-inch pieces; see page 73)

7 ½ cups hot water

2 teaspoons salt

Black pepper, for serving

1 Place the rice in a large bowl. Rinse with warm water, then drain. Repeat two more times, or until the water runs clear. Drain the rice thoroughly in a fine-mesh strainer.

2 Heat the olive and vegetable oils in a large, heavy pot over medium-high until hot. Add the vermicelli and stir to coat with the oil. Cook for 3 to 4 minutes, stirring occasionally, until browned and toasted.

3 Add the rice and stir until thoroughly combined. Cook for 2 to 4 minutes, stirring occasionally, until the rice is lightly toasted. Add the hot water and salt and stir to combine. Bring to a boil on high. Cover and reduce the heat to low. Cook for 40 to 45 minutes, until the rice is fluffy and tender and the water has been absorbed. Transfer to a serving dish and season with pepper before serving.

Bulgur Pilaf with Vermicelli

برغل بالشعيرية

Like Rice Pilaf with Vermicelli (page 70), this dish is a staple side, but with even more earthy flavor from the bulgur. For a more luxurious take, Mayada suggests using ghee (clarified butter) instead of the olive oil.

Vermicelli can be found in Middle Eastern and Latin grocery stores, where it may be referred to as "fideos." Typically, the wheat-based noodles are sold in little nest shapes or already broken up. Do not use Italian vermicelli pasta (it will be too thick) or Asian rice vermicelli (a very different product).

Mayada particularly likes serving this with Chicken and Potato Soup (page 69) and other chicken dishes.

SERVES 6 TO 8

½ cup olive oil

2 cups crumbled wheat vermicelli or fideos (1-inch pieces)

1 quart water

Salt

2 cups coarse bulgur

1 Heat the olive oil in a large pot over medium-high until shimmering. Add the vermicelli and toast for 2 to 3 minutes, stirring occasionally, until lightly browned (it will look almost orange).

2 Carefully add the water (it may splatter) and 2 teaspoons salt. Bring to a boil on high. Stir in the bulgur and reduce the heat to medium. Cover and cook for 15 to 20 minutes, until the bulgur is tender and the water has been absorbed. Fluff with a fork, scraping up any bits that may be stuck to the bottom of the pot. Season with salt to taste and serve immediately.

Every Bulgur Has Its Use

Bulgur is a workhorse ingredient in the Middle Eastern kitchen—showing up in dishes that hail from the Fertile Crescent and beyond, from tabbouleh to kibbeh to pilafs. Made from wheat, most commonly the durum variety, bulgur has a pleasantly nutty flavor and is slightly chewy. Bulgur isn't difficult to find in the United States, but it's helpful to know the differences between the sizes and most common uses.

Bulgur commonly comes in four sizes that denote how finely they're milled: number 1 is the finest and number 4 is the coarsest. While the whole range of bulgur wheat sizes can be found in most Middle Eastern groceries, supermarkets in the United States usually carry numbers 3 and 4. A bit bulkier, they are a great alternative to couscous or rice, as they soak up sauces beautifully. The coarser bulgur is better suited for dishes such as Tabbouleh (page 28), where it can stand up to the parsley, cucumbers, and tomatoes, and soak up dressing. The finer varieties are best for Kibbeh (page 83). If you plan on making Kibbeh and can find only coarse bulgur, don't worry—with a little elbow grease, it forms a malleable dough while retaining its texture.

أكلات ليالي الجمعة و المناسبات
Friday Night Dinners
& Celebrations

Chicken in the Oven with Potatoes

دجاج بالفرن مع البطاطا

Fridays are a special time of the week for Mayada's family, both here and in Homs. In Syria, it was tradition that the whole extended family would gather after Friday prayers to cook and eat—it was the only time each week when everyone got together. Friday mornings, without fail, they would wake up and start cooking for the meal to come, preparing special dishes like this "chicken in the oven" and Mehshi Khodar (page 92). Now, with their family dispersed across Jordan, Turkey, and Lebanon, Mayada and Ahmad still honor their Friday tradition, preparing the same dishes, albeit in smaller amounts.

Mayada explains that many Muslim families enjoy similar roasted chicken meals on Fridays, but, of course, every family does it a little differently. In her version, she marinates chicken pieces in garlic, spices, and vinegar. The chicken is then roasted over potatoes that catch all the drippings and get crispy and brown in the pan. Though she'll switch up the sides, yogurt and a simple salad are mainstays. You can use whichever bone-in chicken parts you prefer (just drumsticks and thighs, for example), or one whole chicken cut into pieces. Mayada removes the skin before cooking, as that's her family's preference.

(recipe continues on page 81)

Chicken in the Oven with Potatoes

SERVES 4 TO 6

3 ½ pounds medium or large russet potatoes

3 pounds bone-in chicken pieces or 1 whole chicken, cut into pieces (skin removed, optional)

¼ cup white vinegar

Olive oil

1 tablespoon tomato paste

3 teaspoons salt

½ teaspoon cayenne pepper

3 ½ tablespoons ground cumin

8 cloves garlic, smashed into a paste with 1 teaspoon salt

1   Peel the potatoes and slice crosswise into ¼-inch-thick rounds. Place in a colander and rinse under cold water. Drain well.

2   Use a small sharp knife to poke several incisions in each chicken piece. Place the chicken in a large bowl and add the vinegar, ¼ cup olive oil, the tomato paste, 1 teaspoon of the salt, ¼ teaspoon of the cayenne, 1½ tablespoons of the cumin, and half of the garlic paste. Use your hands to thoroughly coat the chicken.

3   In a large rimmed baking sheet or roasting pan, combine the potatoes, the remaining ¼ teaspoon cayenne, 2 tablespoons olive oil, 2 tablespoons cumin, remaining garlic paste, and 2 teaspoons salt. Toss to thoroughly coat the potatoes. Spread to evenly cover the pan.

4   Place the chicken pieces on top of the potatoes and pour any marinade remaining in the bowl over the chicken and potatoes. Marinate at room temperature for 30 minutes to 1 hour.

5   While the chicken is marinating, preheat the oven to 425°F.

6   Roast the chicken for about 30 minutes, then check. If the potatoes look dry, lightly drizzle with a little olive oil. Roast for 30 minutes more (about 1 hour total), until the chicken is cooked through. The juices should run clear when you insert a knife, and the potatoes should be crispy and browned. Remove from the oven and let rest for 15 to 20 minutes. Drizzle with additional olive oil before serving.

Kibbeh

كبة

When asked about which recipes she was most excited to share for this book, Mayada reflexively responded, "Well, all of them!" To rank one recipe over another seemed unnatural and perhaps even silly. Yet less than twenty seconds later, with a big smile and a happy look in her eyes, she had a new answer: "The kibbeh. The kibbeh is very, very special." The joy with which she shared the process was palpable.

Kibbeh is famous throughout the Levant but has a particularly special standing in the hearts of Syrians, as many regional versions abound. Mayada sets her basic kibbeh apart by using chicken instead of beef or lamb for the dough, a choice that yields kibbeh lighter in both color and texture. Back in Homs, the men of the family would tackle grinding the meat and bulgur for the dough while the women were tasked with the more intricate job of forming all those kibbeh. The well-earned dexterity, ease, and speed with which Mayada forms each football-shaped dumpling speaks to many years of making countless kibbeh. The walls of her kibbeh are as thin as can be without breaking (a fact that Mayada is quite proud of), creating ample room for the ground beef stuffing. Once fried, those walls form a crunchy but tender crust that reveals the crumbly, savory filling within. (Yes, this is meat stuffed inside meat, and it's incredible.) It certainly is labor-intensive to form and stuff so many, but like most other tasks in Mayada's kitchen, it's a team effort that's enjoyed over an afternoon of Arab music and hot mint tea.

Traditionally, there may be other additions to the stuffing, particularly pine nuts, which Mayada loves; her kids like it without them, but feel free to add some to yours. There is one absolute: kibbeh is a must for any dinner party, and there has to be Tabbouleh (page 28) served by its side.

(recipe continues on next page)

Kibbeh

SERVES 8 TO 10

DOUGH

1 pound fine bulgur (about 2 ¾ cups)

½ pound skinless, boneless chicken breast, cut into 2-inch pieces

¼ onion, sliced

2 teaspoons salt

¼ teaspoon cayenne pepper

STUFFING

2 tablespoons olive oil

½ small onion, coarsely grated

Salt and black pepper

1 pound ground beef (80% lean)

Vegetable oil, for frying

1   Make the dough: Place the bulgur in a large pot or bowl. Add enough hot water to cover. Stir together and let stand for 1 hour, until soft. If the bulgur feels dry, add more hot water and mix until soft; if all the water has not been absorbed, drain off the excess. The bulgur should stick together when pressed into a ball.

2   Add the chicken and onion to the bulgur. Process through a meat grinder with a fine plate two or three times, until very smooth. (You can also use a food processor: Start by chopping the onion. Then, working in batches, add the chicken and bulgur and pulse several times. Stir the mixture and pulse again several times, until a sticky dough begins to form. Do not try to pulse the dough completely smooth in the food processor; it will come out too sticky.)

3   Transfer the mixture to a large bowl. Add the salt and cayenne and mix together with your hand, kneading it until thoroughly combined. Cover the bowl and refrigerate.

4   Make the filling: Heat the olive oil in a large skillet on medium. Add the onion and season with salt and pepper. Cook for 2 to 3 minutes, until softened and translucent. Add the beef and cook for 8 to 10 minutes, until browned and cooked through; frequently stir the beef and break it up with a wooden spoon to create a fine texture. Transfer to a bowl and let cool.

5 To assemble: Fill a small bowl with water to dip your hands in while you work, to prevent sticking. Roll a 2-inch ball of dough between your hands. Use your index finger to form a hole in the center of the ball. Keeping your finger there, roll the bulgur mixture around your finger to form a 3-inch-long hollow cone with very thin sides. (Try not to break the sides.) Wet your hands with water if the dough is sticky.

6 Use a spoon to fill the cone with the beef filling, leaving about ¼ inch from the top of the cone. Pinch and roll the top of the cone closed. With wet hands, turn and shape the kibbeh between your hands to create a torpedo or a football shape, with pointed ends. Transfer to a platter and repeat with the remaining dough and filling.

7 Line a large plate with paper towels. Heat 3 inches of vegetable oil in a large pot on medium-high until hot. Working in batches, add the kibbeh and fry for 12 to 14 minutes, flipping halfway through, until dark brown. Transfer with a slotted spoon to the paper towel–lined plate to drain. Let cool slightly and serve.

Homs and Grilled Kibbeh

Compared to other cities in Syria, Mayada's husband, Ahmad, says, "Homs is filled with people from the countryside, so they are nicer and more tight-knit." The Homsi have a reputation for being the friendliest, most fun Syrians, with a great sense of humor—and Ahmad proves that true. He loves to joke, and today he wants to make sure we know that their family is one of those from the countryside, not from the city. He explains you can tell because they have a slightly different accent. People from Homs proper, he says, are known for being less sophisticated. He tells us about the Mongols and how they came to conquer Syria. The people of Homs decided to act "crazy," stripping off their clothes, so the Mongols would leave them alone. The ruse may not have worked back then, but the reputation stuck.

Outside Homs, in the countryside, Ahmad's grandmother had a home surrounded by beautiful almond and olive trees. Weekend visits there with the family were frequent, and grilled kibbeh, a beloved Homs specialty, was always on the menu. Using practically the same recipe as Mayada's basic kibbeh, you can prepare grilled kibbeh. Simply omit the onion from the dough and shape the kibbeh into flat patties instead of footballs. Grill the patties over charcoal until crisp and lightly charred.

Yogurt Kibbeh

كبة باللبن

How to take a beloved classic kibbeh to even greater heights? Simmer it in a rich, creamy yogurt sauce. When making the sauce, near-constant stirring is needed to prevent the yogurt from separating. Be careful not to leave the finished kibbeh sitting in the hot yogurt sauce for too long; it will break the kibbeh down too far and they'll fall apart. Instead, serve most of the sauce on the side and spoon more as needed onto each person's plate. If you want an extra layer of decadence, coarsely chop a few garlic cloves, fry them in butter until they just start to brown, and pour over the yogurt kibbeh before serving. Mayada always makes basic (page 83) and yogurt kibbeh at the same time so her guests will have both options—plus, her thinking goes, since she's already spending all that time making kibbeh in the first place, why not add another choice?

Note: The ingredients and preparation for the kibbeh is identical to the basic version, except that they're formed into smaller shapes and fried only lightly, not until deeply brown. The more petite size makes the kibbeh more manageable as you simmer them (and less prone to falling apart), and the lighter shell allows the yogurt sauce to envelop and soak into the dumplings. Follow the recipe for Kibbeh (page 83), but in Step 6, form smaller shapes (start with a 1½-inch ball of dough and make a 2½-inch cone), and fry for only 6 minutes, until lightly browned.

SERVES 8 TO 10

Kibbeh (page 83)

1 quart plain whole-milk yogurt (not Greek)

1 teaspoon salt

1 egg, beaten

2 cups water

1   Prepare and cook the kibbeh according to the Note.

2   In a large pot, combine the yogurt, salt, and egg; stir until thoroughly mixed. Add the water and stir until combined.

3   Heat the yogurt sauce on medium-high, stirring constantly so the yogurt doesn't separate, until simmering. Add the kibbeh and cook for 10 minutes, gently stirring occasionally. Transfer the kibbeh to a serving dish and top with some of the sauce. Transfer the remaining sauce to a serving bowl and serve on the side. Do not leave the kibbeh in the pot of hot yogurt, as they'll fall apart.

Stuffed Vegetables

محشي خضار (يالنجي)   MEHSHI KHODAR (YALINGY)

Back in Homs, making stuffed vegetables, or *mehshi*, was an all-day affair that created enough meals for days to come. It was common for Mayada to sit down to a kitchen table loaded with more than twenty pounds of vegetables, a mix of eggplants and zucchini, all waiting to be cored and stuffed. Today, she's happy to have extra helping hands, but even so, several pounds of vegetables in, Mayada points to her biceps and laughs at how sore it is: "Are we going to relax after this? My arm is tired!" The key to Mayada's *mehshi* is how thinly she hollows out each eggplant or zucchini, which takes a lot of skill honed over many, many pounds of vegetables. She deftly turns each vegetable in her hand as the long, slender corer (an essential tool in Middle Eastern kitchens) does its work, hardly ever piercing through the skin; when it does, she exclaims a big "Uh oh!" and shakes her head in disappointment, laughing all the while. The thin shell creates *mehshi* that have ample room for its rice stuffing, but with less flesh that can become waterlogged. How thin she gets her *mehshi* is a source of pride; at a later occasion, she quietly mentions that not many people can make their *mehshi* as thin as she can.

While the vegetables slowly simmer in the tomato sauce, there's coffee to enjoy and only the easy, fast Sauteed Zucchini Hearts (page 99) to prepare. No other side dishes are needed for the table—a rare occurrence. As Mayada points out, the *mehshi* has everything you need—vegetables, rice, and meat—so although the process creates some aching arms, there's some reprieve to be had.

Note: Mayada goes to her specialty Middle Eastern grocery store to buy small zucchini and eggplant varieties for her *mehshi*. Though slightly larger zucchini can work (they'll be a bit harder to core), large globe eggplants won't; if you can't find small round eggplants, look for slender Japanese or short fairy-tale eggplants. Make sure not to trim the zucchini bottoms too far—just a sliver—or else there won't be a sturdy bottom when you hollow the center and you'll find your corer too easily piercing through. To enclose the open end of the vegetables, you can use the zucchini top, a small piece of tomato, or even small bunched-up scraps of grape leaves. Once the vegetables and filling are cooked through, immediately transfer them to a serving platter. If they stand in the pot of hot tomato sauce for too long, they'll get too soft and burst.

(recipe continues on page 94)

SERVES 10 TO 12

1½ pounds small long eggplants, about 5 inches long (see Note)

2 pounds small round eggplants (see Note)

6 pounds small zucchini, about 5 inches long

¼ cup crushed dried mint leaves

Meat Filling (recipe follows)

¼ cup olive oil

One 12-ounce can tomato paste (1½ cups)

1 teaspoon salt

1   Cut off the tops of the eggplants. Cut off and reserve the tops of the zucchini and trim the bottoms slightly. Use a coring tool to hollow out the inside of the eggplants and zucchini (reserve the zucchini "hearts"), creating a thin exterior shell but being careful not to pierce the skin.

2   Fill a large bowl with water and mint. Working in batches, place a few zucchini in the water, swish around to coat with mint, drain, and transfer to a platter.

3   Use your fingers to stuff each eggplant and zucchini with the filling about halfway. Use the reserved zucchini tops (trimmed, if too large) to plug the openings so the filling does not fall out, being careful not to split the vegetables.

4   Line the bottom of a large pot with a single even layer of eggplant. Repeat with the remaining eggplant. Layer the zucchini on top. Add enough water to almost cover (the top layer of zucchini should be halfway covered with water).

5   Heat the olive oil in a small pot on medium-high. Add the tomato paste and salt. Cook for 1 to 2 minutes, stirring frequently, until thoroughly mixed and just heated through.

6   Spread the tomato sauce on top of the zucchini. Cover and bring to a boil on high. Boil for about 5 minutes, then reduce the heat to medium-low. Place a heavy heatproof plate on top of the zucchini to keep the vegetables submerged while cooking. Cover the pot and cook for about 1½ hours, until the meat is cooked through and the rice is tender (remove one of the zucchini to check).

7   Using tongs or a slotted spoon, immediately transfer the zucchini and eggplants to a serving platter, being careful not to break the skins. Transfer the tomato sauce to a serving bowl and serve alongside the vegetables.

MEAT FILLING

For the rice, you may use medium-grain instead of short-grain, but never long-grain.

STUFFS ABOUT 10 POUNDS VEGETABLES AND ONE 2-POUND JAR GRAPE LEAVES

3 ¼ cups short-grain white rice

1 pound ground beef (80% lean)

4 large cloves garlic, smashed into a paste with ½ teaspoon salt

½ cup olive oil

1 tablespoon salt

1 tablespoon black pepper

1½ tablespoons crushed dried mint leaves

1 tablespoon unsalted butter, softened

Place the rice in a large pot or bowl and add enough warm water to cover. Let soak for 30 minutes. Drain, then rinse until the water runs clear. Drain thoroughly and return to the pot. Add the beef, garlic paste, olive oil, salt, pepper, mint, and butter. Use your hands to thoroughly mix together. Cover and refrigerate until needed.

Serving Mehshi

⁖⟨⟡⟨⟡⟩⟡⟩⁖

When the *mehshi* is ready, Mayada transfers the vegetables to a platter and everyone gets a bowl of tomato sauce on the side. Each person at the table has his or her own way of digging in. Mayada and her husband both tear large swaths of Syrian flatbread and use it to pick up one zucchini or eggplant at a time, wrapping it up a like a burrito—"It's a Syrian thing," they say, with big smiles. The tomato sauce is enjoyed separately, a few spoonfuls sipped at a time between bites of their bread-wrapped *mehshi*. A neighborhood friend who hails from Palestine, however, plucks a vegetable from the pile with her hand and eats it as is: "This is how we do it back home in Palestine," she announces. Dalia, the translator, eats hers a third way, breaking open the vegetable with a spoon and drizzling the tomato sauce over the inside, soaking the rice. Mayada notices and remarks that she's happy to learn a new way to eat *mehshi* and tries it herself. Though the day began with Mayada telling everyone how excited the kids are that she's making one of their all-time favorite dishes, when she calls the boys to the table, they shout back that they're too full from eating pizza after their soccer match.

Sauteed Zucchini Hearts

لب الكوسا

In Mayada's kitchen, nothing goes to waste, especially when making Mehshi Khodar (page 92). The zucchini "hearts" you worked so diligently to hollow from your squash form the base of this easy side, turning silky and luscious in the garlic and oil. It's the perfect mezze to tuck into with pita as you wait for your *mehshi* to finish cooking.

SERVES 4 TO 6

3 tablespoons olive oil

4 cloves garlic, coarsely chopped

About 3 cups leftover zucchini hearts, cut into 1-inch pieces, drained of excess water

1 teaspoon salt

¼ teaspoon black pepper

2 teaspoons crushed dried mint leaves

1 Heat the oil in a medium pot on medium-low. Add the garlic and cook 1 minute, until beginning to soften and lightly brown. Add the zucchini, salt, pepper, and mint. Stir until combined.

2 Cover and cook for 10 to 15 minutes, until the zucchini is softened and just cooked through. Uncover and cook about 5 minutes more, until most of the water is evaporated. Let cool slightly and serve.

Stuffed Grape Leaves

محشي ورق عنب   MEHSHI WARAQ ENAB

Like many of Mayada's most prized dishes, this one requires a deft touch and, most important, patience. Soon enough you'll be rewarded with tender grape leaves stuffed with rice and beef that will disappear in a fraction of the time it took to roll them. When forming the stuffed leaves, you may be faced with a seemingly insurmountable amount of filling to use up, but resist the urge to overstuff your leaves to get through the filling faster. Remember that the rice will expand, and if the leaves are overstuffed or rolled too tightly, those logs you worked so hard to roll will burst. (Mayada's version is thinner, more of a slender pinky than the fat thumb-like Greek dolmades.) They're ready to come out of the pot when the rice is cooked and the leaves are very tender—Mayada says that the leaves should give easily between your teeth when you take a bite.

SERVES 8 TO 10

One 2-pound jar grape leaves

Meat Filling (page 95)

1 head garlic, skin on, cut in half crosswise

2 teaspoons salt

¼ cup olive oil

1   Drain the leaves and place in a large pot. Add enough water to cover and bring to a boil on high. Reduce the heat to medium and simmer for 10 minutes. Drain well and transfer to a platter. Let cool slightly before rolling.

2   Working one at a time, spread a leaf flat on a cutting board, veined side up. Place about 1 teaspoon of the filling in a short line across the bottom of the leaf (more or less, depending on the size of the leaf). Fold the bottom of the leaf up over the filling, then fold in the right and left sides of the leaf. Snugly roll up the leaf (like a burrito) and set aside on a platter. Repeat with the remaining grape leaves and filling.

3   Line the bottom of a large pot with the stuffed grape leaves in even layers, tightly packing them in. Place each succeeding layer of leaves at a right angle to the one below.

4   Add enough water to cover by ½ inch. Top with the garlic, salt, and olive oil. Cover, bring to a boil on high, and boil for 5 minutes. Reduce the heat to medium-low. After 15 minutes, add additional water to cover. Place a heavy heatproof plate on top of the grape leaves to keep them submerged while cooking. Cover and simmer for about 2 ½ hours, until the leaves are very tender. (Keep checking; the leaves should be very soft and almost melting. This will depend on the leaves you get, as some are tougher than others.) Use a slotted spoon to transfer to a serving platter. Discard the garlic and leftover cooking liquid. Let cool and serve.

Spiced Chicken with Rice

كبسة   **KABSA**

Chicken *kabsa*, a dish with roots in the Persian Gulf region, is a Friday night favorite at Mayada's, especially among the kids—even Jana, Mayada says. (On this Friday night, Jana is singing songs and banging on her brothers' bedroom door with a big spatula. Once she makes her way in, screeching ensues, and she's swiftly booted out, much to her dismay.)

Mayada finishes the dish using a special technique that nods to the traditional *mandi* cooking style, in which the meat and rice are cooked in *taboon* clay ovens. Similar to tandoor ovens, they're built in the ground and tightly sealed so no smoke can escape. In New Jersey, with no underground oven in sight, Mayada lights charcoal on her stovetop and nestles the glowing lumps in the pots of chicken and rice to infuse them with heady, smoky flavor.

Mayada uses drumsticks because they're Hayan's favorite, but you can use any chicken parts or even a whole chicken cut into pieces. (The other boys actually love the rice itself more than the chicken, which often remains untouched on their plates.) Mayada always serves yogurt on the side, its cooling effect bringing a welcome balance to the smokiness.

Note: Sumac—not to be confused with poison sumac—is a deep red, lemony-tasting spice of ground dried berries. It's available in Middle Eastern stores and online, along with the spice mix, sometimes called *baharat*. Do not use charcoal briquettes that have been infused with lighter fluid (sometimes called "Match Light"). If you don't have a gas stove or want to avoid the charcoal step because of the smoke, feel free to omit.

(recipe continues on next page)

Spiced Chicken with Rice

SERVES 8 TO 10

KABSA SPICE

1 tablespoon ground coriander

1 tablespoon black pepper

2 teaspoons ground cardamom

2 teaspoons ground cinnamon

1 teaspoon ground cloves

½ teaspoon ground nutmeg

1 teaspoon sumac (see Note)

CHICKEN

1 tablespoon ground turmeric

1 tablespoon salt

2 tablespoons plain whole-milk yogurt (not Greek)

2 tablespoons tomato paste

5 dried bay leaves

5 cardamom pods, crushed

⅓ cup olive oil

1 small onion, thinly sliced

10 small chicken drumsticks (about 3 pounds)

1 Make the kabsa spice: Place all the ingredients in a small jar. Cap tightly and shake to combine.

2 Make the chicken: Preheat the oven to 400°F. In a large bowl, stir together 2 tablespoons of the kabsa spice, the turmeric, salt, yogurt, tomato paste, bay leaves, cardamom, and olive oil. Add the onion and chicken and toss until the chicken is thoroughly coated. Transfer the chicken, onion, and marinade to a 9-by-13-inch baking dish and spread in a single layer. Cover with foil. Bake for 30 minutes. Remove from the oven and flip the chicken pieces. Return to the oven, uncovered. Bake for 15 to 20 minutes more, until deeply browned and cooked through. Remove and discard the bay leaves and cardamom pods. Transfer the chicken and sauce to a large pot or Dutch oven and keep warm.

3 While the chicken bakes uncovered, make the rice: Rinse the rice four or five times, until the water runs clear. Drain thoroughly. Heat 1 cup vegetable oil in a large pot on medium-high. Add the onion, green pepper, and garlic and cook for 3 to 4 minutes, until softened. Stir in the remaining kabsa spice, the turmeric, 1 teaspoon of the salt, and the tomatoes. Cover and cook for about 5 minutes, until the tomatoes break down. Add the hot water and the remaining 1 teaspoon salt. Bring to a boil on medium-high, then gently stir in the rice. Return to a boil, then reduce the heat to medium-low. Cover and cook for 20 minutes, stirring after 10 minutes, until the rice is tender and the liquid has been absorbed. Remove from the heat and keep warm.

RICE

3 cups white basmati rice, soaked in water for 1 hour and drained

1 cup vegetable oil, plus 4 tablespoons for the charcoal

1 small onion, coarsely grated

½ green bell pepper, coarsely grated

1 clove garlic, coarsely chopped

1 tablespoon ground turmeric

2 teaspoons salt

2 medium-large tomatoes (about 1 ¼ pounds), halved and coarsely grated, skin discarded

5 cups hot water

4   Set a wire rack over a gas burner. Place 3 charcoal briquettes on top of the rack and heat on high until the coals are lit and glowing, with a thin layer of ash.

5   Use a large spoon to make an indentation in the center of the rice. Place a 6-inch square of foil in the indentation, to make a basket. Very carefully place 2 of the briquettes on the foil. Immediately pour 2 tablespoons vegetable oil over the briquettes. Quickly cover the pot to trap the smoke.

6   Place a 6-inch square of foil in the center of the chicken to make a basket. Very carefully place the remaining briquette in the foil. Immediately pour the remaining 2 tablespoons vegetable oil over the briquette. Quickly cover the pot to trap the smoke.

7   Let the rice and chicken stand for 5 to 10 minutes to infuse them with smoke. Uncover and very carefully remove the foil and briquettes. Set them aside on a heatproof surface to cool. When cold, dispose of the briquettes safely.

8   Transfer the rice to a serving platter. Top with the chicken and serve.

Chicken, Vegetables, and Rice

مقلوبة   MAQLUBA

Maqluba, which means "upside down" in Arabic, is a traditional dish made of meat, vegetables, and rice that gets its name from how it's traditionally served—flipped onto a platter and unmolded, revealing all its layers like the most delicious, savory cake. For Mayada's family, *maqluba* is often served on Friday nights, though they prefer less showmanship. Her kids don't like the layers and ask for it all mixed up, so before the ingredients all cook together, she gives the pot a couple of big stirs.

Mayada uses chicken breasts, but she advises that other chicken parts, such as chicken thighs (bone-in or boneless), will work. The eggplants in Syria tend to be smaller than the large globe eggplants you'll find here in most supermarkets; if you come upon smaller varieties, feel free to use them.

Her kids have one last request that you can follow, too, if you like: The eggplant is first fried and then simmered until very soft, because they also don't like to see any discernible eggplant pieces in the dish. This way, the eggplant practically melts, disappearing into the rice and suffusing its flavor throughout.

Note: For a layered presentation, do not stir the layers together at all. To serve, place a large serving dish on top of the pot; very carefully, invert the pot.

(recipe continues on page 114)

SERVES 8 TO 10

2 pounds eggplant, peeled and cut into 1½-inch cubes

Salt and black pepper

1½ pounds skinless, boneless chicken breasts or thighs, cut in half

½ small onion, thinly sliced

2 cardamom pods, crushed

3 dried bay leaves

4 tablespoons olive oil

2 ½ cups medium-grain white rice

Vegetable oil

Cucumber Yogurt (page 31), for serving

1   Place the eggplant in a large bowl and season with about 1½ teaspoons salt. Toss to combine.

2   Place the chicken in a large pot and add enough water to cover. Add the onion, cardamom, bay leaves, 2 tablespoons of the olive oil, 1 teaspoon salt, and ½ teaspoon pepper. Cover and bring to a boil on high. Reduce the heat to low and simmer for 20 to 25 minutes, until the chicken is cooked through and tender. Use a slotted spoon to transfer the chicken and onion to a large plate. Remove and discard the bay leaves and cardamom. Set aside the pot with the broth. Let the chicken stand until cool enough to handle. Once cooled, use your fingers to pull the chicken into large bite-size pieces (about 1½ inches).

3   While the chicken is cooking, in a large bowl, combine the rice and ½ teaspoon salt. Add enough warm water to cover. Soak for 20 minutes. Drain.

4   Heat ½ inch of vegetable oil in a large skillet on high until hot. Working in batches, add the eggplant in a single layer and fry for 8 to 10 minutes, flipping it halfway through, until deeply browned all over. Use a slotted spoon to transfer the eggplant to the chicken broth. Repeat with the remaining eggplant. (If you prefer your eggplant in more discernible pieces, do not transfer the eggplant to the broth. Skip to Step 6 after browning all the eggplant.)

5   Bring the pot of eggplant and broth to a boil on high. Reduce the heat to low and simmer for 20 minutes, until the eggplant is very soft. Place a fine-mesh strainer or colander over a large bowl and drain the eggplant. Reserve the broth.

6   Return the pot to the stove and heat 2 tablespoons olive oil and 2 tablespoons vegetable oil on high. Add one-third of the eggplant in a single layer. Top with one-third of the chicken, in a single layer. Top with one-third of the rice and spread it in a layer. Repeat layering twice more with the remaining eggplant, chicken, and rice. Smooth the top. Stir together 3 ¾ cups broth (if you don't have enough, supplement it with water), 1 teaspoon salt, and ½ teaspoon pepper, and gently pour it into the pot. Stir everything together. Cover, bring to a boil on medium-high, then stir again and reduce the heat to medium-low.

7   Cook, covered, for 25 to 30 minutes, until the rice is tender and the liquid has been absorbed. Transfer to a serving platter. Serve with the Cucumber Yogurt on the side.

Chicken Stew with Jew's Mallow

The name of both the dish and the leafy greens in it, *mulukhiyah* and its many iterations are famous, especially in Egypt. The highly nutritious plant, also known as "Jew's mallow" or "jute mallow," has an earthy, slightly bitter taste when cooked and can produce a thick, viscous liquid, similar to okra, to which the plant is related. Rinsing and wringing the leaves well helps reduce the plant's bitterness and gets rid of much of the thick liquid.

Mulukhiyah can be found dried or frozen in Middle Eastern and Asian grocery stores. When it comes to these specialty ingredients, Mayada says, "Everything I need is here. I can make anything I want to make—no problems." Learning to navigate the New Jersey public transportation system was a big help. When she first arrived at her new home in the States, she says, "it took me about five months to discover all the places to shop. The first few months, I didn't know how to ride the bus, so we would just walk! We'd walk for one hour to the store. We'd find a little garden, take a rest, and then continue."

Mayada's Syrian version of *mulukhiyah* uses whole dried leaves that are first rehydrated before they are stewed with chicken, broth, coriander, and lots of garlic. It's finished with a generous amount of fresh lemon juice that balances the deep, heady flavor of the leaf. Using *mulukhiyah* leaves whole, rather than chopped very fine as in the soupier Egyptian version, creates a heartier—and less viscous—texture. Since the dish is somewhat time-consuming to prepare, Mayada reserves it for more special occasions, but particularly ones in winter, as it's warming and comforting.

(recipe continues on page 118)

Chicken Stew with Jew's Mallow

SERVES 6 TO 8

8 ounces dried mulukhiyah leaves

1 pound skinless, boneless chicken breast

½ small onion, sliced

3 dried bay leaves

Salt

3 tablespoons olive oil

3 cardamom pods, lightly crushed

1 tablespoon vegetable oil

4 large cloves garlic, smashed into a paste with ¾ teaspoon salt

1½ tablespoons ground coriander

¼ teaspoon cayenne pepper

Juice of 1 lemon, plus extra lemon wedges for serving

1 Bring a large pot of water to a boil. Stir in the mulukhiyah leaves, remove from the heat, cover, and set aside for 2 hours to rehydrate.

2 Meanwhile, cook the chicken: In a small pot, combine the chicken breast, onion, bay leaves, 1 teaspoon salt, 1 table-spoon of the olive oil, the cardamom, and enough water just to cover the meat. Set over medium-high and bring to a boil. Reduce the heat to medium-low and simmer for 18 to 20 min-utes, until the chicken is cooked through. Transfer the chicken to a large plate to cool. Strain and reserve the broth separately.

3 When the chicken is cool enough to handle, tear it into large bite-size shreds.

4 Set a colander in the sink. Drain the leaves and let drip for 15 minutes. Rinse out the pot. Rinse the leaves with cold water, tossing them under the running water with your hands. Let stand in the colander for 10 minutes more for the excess water to drip away. Using your hands and working in batches, squeeze the leaves dry, removing as much of the viscous liquid as possible.

5 Set the pot back over medium-high heat and add the remaining 2 tablespoons olive oil and the vegetable oil. When the oil is hot, add the garlic paste and cook for about 1 minute, until lightly browned. Add the chicken and stir until well coated. Stir in the coriander, cayenne, and ½ teaspoon salt and cook for a few seconds, stirring, until the spices are very fragrant. Add the leaves and stir until they are well coated in the spice mixture. Reduce the heat to medium-low. Stir in 1 cup of the reserved broth, cover, and cook for 20 to 25 minutes, stirring occasionally, until the leaves are very tender. Uncover, stir in the lemon juice, and cook for 3 to 5 minutes, until most of the liquid has evaporated. Season with salt to taste and serve with extra lemon wedges on the side.

Dinners with Mayada

For many refugees, getting to the United States—a seemingly improbable feat in itself—is only the beginning of a long journey to building a new life. As Mayada's family's cosponsors, the Rutgers Presbyterian Church's Refugee Task Force helped facilitate the initial process of resettlement and has remained key in the vital transition that followed and continues. As Nancy Muirhead, the chair of the task force recalls, "Upon arrival in the US, Mayada and her family not only had to learn a new language and culture, but also had to find ways to earn income. Refugees typically receive only a few months of modest financial support from the US government and refugee resettlement agencies, so there is immediate pressure to find employment or income-generating activities."

Since Mayada is such an excellent cook, the task force, inspired by a *New York Times* article about similar events in Berlin, came up with the idea of hosting fund-raising dinners cooked by Mayada, assisted by volunteers. All proceeds from the dinners go toward supporting Mayada and her family, and now Mayada hosts dinners beyond Rutgers for other faith-based communities. "The dinners have helped raise awareness about refugees and nurture new connections and bonds among people in New York City who want to help in some way," Nancy says.

The sold-out dinners were a great success for Mayada, in more ways than one. Nancy recalls, "Mayada has spoken at each dinner, her confidence growing with each event. She's used the proceeds from the dinners to purchase a car, so her husband, Ahmad, can drive to his job each day. She proudly said at one of the dinners that Ahmad can use the car, but she earned it!"

Falafel

فلافل

At her very first dinner at Rutgers Presbyterian Church, with a sold-out crowd of seventy-five guests, Mayada served these falafel, among many other dishes. It was her first time cooking for so many people, and feeling a bit nervous, she ended up making much more than was needed.

Falafel are well loved and ubiquitous throughout the Middle East, with many regional variations. Mayada's simple version uses chickpeas with the addition of parsley, shallot, cumin, and coriander. Many traditional shops and homes use a falafel press, a special tool for molding and dispensing the falafel into the hot oil. If using the press, push the mixture into the mold and form a generous ¾-inch mound on top. You can always use your hands to shape the falafel if you don't have a press—either way, remember that if the patty is too thin, the falafel will be overly dry. Make sure the oil is hot enough before you start frying; if not, the falafel will be grease-logged instead of crispy.

Mayada uses a meat grinder to make the dough, but you can use a food processor if you have one. Serve as is or with pita, sliced tomatoes and onion, and lettuce.

SERVES 8 TO 10

1 pound dried chickpeas (2 cups), soaked overnight and drained

1 large shallot, cut into quarters

1 cup parsley leaves and tender stems, loosely packed (about ⅔ small bunch)

2 teaspoons salt

2 teaspoons ground cumin

2 teaspoons ground coriander

1 teaspoon baking soda

Vegetable oil, for frying

Tahini Sauce, for serving (optional)

1 Combine the chickpeas, shallot, and parsley in a food processor and process until very fine. Alternatively, use a meat grinder and let it fall into a large bowl.

2 Add the salt, cumin, coriander, and baking soda. Mix or process until thoroughly combined.

3 Line a large plate with paper towels. Heat 2 inches of vegetable oil in a large pot on medium-high until hot. Test a small piece of dough; the oil should start bubbling immediately. Lightly wet your hands and form the dough into 1½-inch balls. Slightly flatten the balls and make an indentation in the middle with your finger. (Alternatively, use a falafel press.)

4   Working in batches, add the falafel to the hot oil and cook for 3 to 4 minutes on each side, flipping once, until browned on both sides. Use a slotted spoon to transfer the falafel to the paper towels to drain. Repeat with the remaining falafel dough. Serve immediately, with Tahini Sauce on the side (if using).

TAHINI SAUCE

ABOUT 2 CUPS

1 cup tahini

¼ cup fresh lemon juice

¾ cup cold water

1 clove garlic, finely chopped or grated (optional)

⅔ cup chopped parsley, leaves and tender stems (about ½ small bunch)

1½ teaspoons salt

In a medium bowl, stir together the tahini and lemon juice. Slowly stir in the cold water (the consistency should be loose and saucy). Stir in the garlic (if using), parsley, and salt.

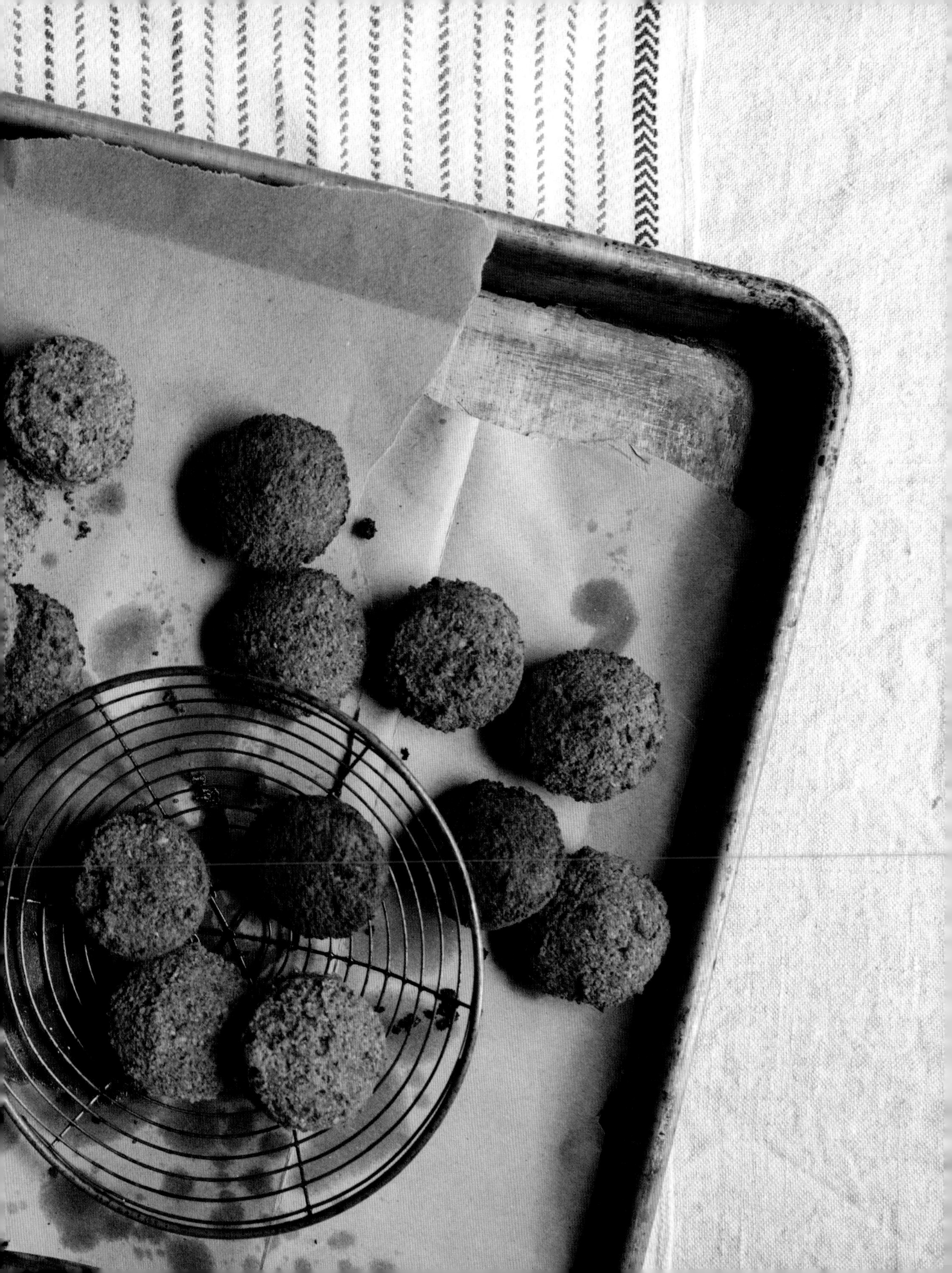

Spinach-Stuffed Pies

سمبوسك   SPINACH FATAYER

These tender, savory pies, popular throughout the Middle East, are a favorite in Mayada's home, especially for parties when she'll prepare them with all of her favorite fillings: meat with onion, spinach, and cheese. She learned to make *fatayer* from her mother, and they'd have tea, chatting and gossiping, while they cooked. "Whenever we're having a dinner or get-together, you always have to have an appetizer, and this is one of my favorites. My kids love it so much that I sometimes make it as a main dish," she says. Although she's made this dough countless times, she says, "Once I start measuring, it gets messed up; when I don't, it's perfect." Proofing the dough in an area of your house that's not drafty is key—Mayada covers her bowl with a plastic bag and whisks it off to her sons' closet, where it's warmer. For Mayada, less is more when it comes to the filling: "Some people overstuff their *fatayer* or make them very big, but I think they taste better when they're smaller and with less."

With hospitality always on her mind, Mayada suggests always making extra *fatayer* so you can freeze them to have on hand for unexpected guests. If she has any dough left over, Mayada likes to make za'atar flatbread. She rolls the dough out flat and slathers it with a mixture of za'atar (a mix of dried thyme, oregano, toasted sesame seeds, and sumac) and olive oil before baking.

When asked how many *fatayer* this recipe makes, she answers, "When you count something, they say it takes away its blessing." So instead, we talk about how many people her recipe will feed. "Served with other dishes, it will feed about fifteen people. Or actually thirteen, because people in the Arab world love to eat."

(recipe continues on next page)

Spinach-Stuffed Pies

SERVES 12 TO 16

DOUGH

1 scant teaspoon active dry yeast, or half a ¼ oz package yeast

1 tablespoon plus 1 teaspoon sugar

¼ cup warm water

6 cups all-purpose flour, plus more if needed

1 tablespoon salt

1½ cups whole milk, lukewarm

¼ cup vegetable oil, plus more for the pans and shaping

FILLING

½ cup olive oil

Two 10 oz packages frozen chopped spinach, thawed and thoroughly drained

1 teaspoon salt

½ teaspoon cayenne pepper

1 Make the dough: In a small bowl, combine the yeast, sugar, and the warm water. Stir together and let stand for 5 to 10 minutes, until foamy.

2 In a large bowl, combine the flour and salt. Add the dissolved yeast, milk, and oil. Use your hand to gradually mix the liquid into the dry ingredients. The dough will be soft and slightly sticky.

3 Remove the dough from the bowl; grease the bowl and the ball of dough and replace it in the bowl. Cover with plastic wrap and set aside in a warm place for about 30 minutes (or in a cool place for 1 hour), until the dough has risen to twice its size.

4 While the dough rises, make the filling: Heat the olive oil in a medium pot on medium-high. Add the spinach, salt, and cayenne. Stir, coating the spinach in the oil. Reduce the heat to medium-low. Cover and cook for 20 minutes, until very soft. Transfer the filling to a bowl to cool.

5 Preheat the oven to 400°F. Lightly oil 2 large rimmed baking sheets and the center of a cutting board. Working in batches and leaving the rest of the dough covered as you work, pull off a small piece (about a 1½-inch ball) and place it on the oiled part of the cutting board. Use a rolling pin to roll it into

a 4-inch circle (it doesn't have to be perfectly round), turning and flipping the dough as needed. Place 1 tablespoon of the spinach filling in the center of the circle and pat it down slightly. Fold one side of the dough over the filling so that only an edge of filling peeks through. Fold a second side of the dough over the filling (the fatayer will have three sides), overlapping with the previous fold, to make the second side of the triangle. Fold the last side of the triangle over the filling. The sides should overlap slightly and no filling should peek through. Lightly press the seams with your fingers to seal. Carefully transfer to a baking sheet. Repeat with the remaining dough and filling.

6 Bake for 10 to 15 minutes, until lightly browned on top and bottom. Let cool, then transfer to a serving platter.

Meat-Stuffed Pies

فطائر باللحمة   **MEAT FATAYER**

This meat with onion *fatayer* variation is one that Mayada's sons love. Mayada says you can also use lamb, which can be a bit richer, or a combination of beef and lamb. Unlike the spinach *fatayer*, which are folded into triangle shapes, meat *fatayer* get a half-moon treatment.

SERVES 12 TO 16

2 tablespoons olive oil

1 small onion, coarsely grated

1½ pounds ground beef (80% lean)

Salt and pepper

Vegetable oil, for the pans and shaping the dough

Dough from Spinach Fatayer (page 126)

1 Heat the olive oil in a large skillet on medium-high until hot. Add the onion and cook for 3 to 5 minutes, until softened. Add the beef and season generously with salt and pepper. Use a wooden spoon or a heat-proof spatula to fold the onion into the beef as it cooks, frequently pressing the beef down and breaking it up to a fine texture. Cook for 10 to 15 minutes, until the meat is cooked through and almost all of the liquid has evaporated. Drain the excess fat and set aside to cool.

2 Preheat the oven to 400°F. Lightly oil 2 large rimmed baking sheets. Working in batches and leaving the rest of the dough covered as you work, pull off a handful of dough (about a 2 ½-inch ball), flatten it slightly with your hands, and place on an oiled cutting board. Use a rolling pin to roll the dough to ⅛- to ¼-inch thick, in a general circular shape (it doesn't have to be perfectly round), turning and flipping the dough as needed. Spoon 1 tablespoon of the meat filling onto the center of the circle; use a slotted spoon to leave any rendered fat behind in the bowl. Fold the dough over the filling to make a half-moon shape. Use your fingers to firmly seal the dough, then use a fork to crimp around the edges. Carefully transfer to a baking sheet. Repeat with the remaining dough and filling, recombining the scraps of dough to roll out more fatayer.

3 Bake for 12 to 15 minutes, until lightly browned on top and bottom. Let cool, then transfer to a serving platter.

Cheese Fingers

:⠿⠿⠿⠿⠿:

Two-year-old Jana struts into any room like a tiny Godzilla ready to destroy all that lies before her—sure, she's really cute with giant dimples and a mop of chestnut curls, but a Godzilla, regardless. With Jana in the kitchen, any bowl of ingredients is literally up for grabs, ready to be dumped on the floor with relish. With her big brothers at home on summer break from school, Jana trails behind them, right at their heels, her little hand wriggling doorknobs of bedrooms and bathrooms swiftly shut before she can enter. When those bowls stay put and the doors remain closed, crying inevitably ensues. One of the quickest ways to soothe those tears is her favorite song, a nursery rhyme called "Finger Family" that gets played on repeat. She is, undoubtedly, the queen of the household, melting everyone's hearts with her big smile. The family's cosponsors joke that she'll end up with a Jersey accent, but Mayada and Ahmad are thrilled that she'll grow up learning both English and Arabic (right now, she knows more English than the latter).

Whenever Mayada makes spinach or meat *fatayer*, she's bound to put aside some of the dough to make a cheese version beloved by all her kids, especially Jana. Mayada calls them "cheese fingers" because of their fun, easy-to-eat shape. It may be just a coincidence, but along with the "Finger Family" song, these cheese fingers are another surefire way to bring a smile to Jana's face.

Mayada uses the popular French cream cheese Kiri (marketed to children, but nostalgically loved by adults too) or Laughing Cow cheese to stuff her *fatayer*, but your own favorite cream cheese will do just fine.

To make Mayada's cheese fingers, cut cold cream cheese into 1-tablespoon pieces. Using dough from Spinach Fatayer (page 126), pull off a piece (about a 2 ½-inch ball) and place it on the oiled part of the cutting board. Use a rolling pin to roll it into a 6-inch circle (it doesn't have to be perfectly round), turning and flipping the dough as needed. Cut the circle in half. Use a sharp knife to cut vertical slits about 1 ½ inches long through the top half of the half-moon. Place 1 tablespoon of the cream cheese below the slits. Roll the dough up and over the cream cheese and form a tube like a thick cigar, leaving the ends open. Repeat with more dough and cream cheese and transfer to a lightly oiled baking sheet. Bake in a preheated 400°F oven for 10 to 12 minutes, until lightly browned on top and bottom. Let cool before serving.

Fatteh with Hummus

فتة حُمُّص

In the Levant, *fatteh* refers to the type of casseroles that involve layered, torn-up flatbread (*fatteh* comes from the Arabic word for "torn bread"). Mayada's version with hummus and yogurt is a filling, comforting dish that's certainly rich but also easy on the stomach—perfect for breaking the fast during Ramadan. Fried pieces of pita are soaked in a mixture of spiced hummus and yogurt that's studded with whole chickpeas. The game-changing touch is the sizzling-hot topping of ghee and garlic—don't skip this step. Though her kids prefer the dish without it, another traditional addition is a final sprinkle of toasted pine nuts.

SERVES 6 TO 8

½ pound dried chickpeas (1 cup), soaked overnight and drained

½ teaspoon baking soda

Vegetable oil, for frying

1 large pita, split and torn into 2-inch pieces

¾ cup plain whole-milk yogurt (not Greek)

½ tablespoon salt

1 teaspoon ground cumin

Juice of ½ lemon

1½ tablespoons tahini

2 tablespoons ghee

1 clove garlic, coarsely chopped

Cayenne pepper, for serving

⅓ cup pine nuts, toasted (optional)

1 Place the chickpeas in a large pot and add enough water to cover by 2 inches. Stir in the baking soda. Bring to a boil on high, then reduce the heat to medium. Cook until soft and cooked through; depending on how old the chickpeas are, this can take between 30 minutes and 2 hours. If the water gets low, add more to cover the chickpeas by 2 inches. Turn off the heat and let the chickpeas cool in the cooking liquid.

2 Line a large plate with paper towels. Heat 2 inches of vegetable oil in a large pot on medium-high until hot. Add the pita and fry for 2 to 3 minutes total, flipping once, until deep golden brown on both sides. Transfer to the paper towels to drain.

(recipe continues on next page)

Fatteh with Hummus

3   Drain the chickpeas and reserve 1½ cups of the cooking liquid. Working in batches if necessary, combine 2 ½ cups of the chickpeas, ¾ cup of the cooking liquid, the yogurt, salt, cumin, lemon juice, and tahini in a blender. Blend until very smooth. Transfer to a bowl.

4   Add ¼ cup of the remaining chickpeas. Stir in a few tablespoons of the cooking liquid to achieve the consistency of thick pancake batter.

5   Spread the pita chips in an even layer in a 9-by-13-inch baking dish or rimmed serving platter. Drizzle with ½ cup of the cooking liquid. Pour the chickpea-yogurt mixture over the chips. Top with the remaining whole chickpeas. (Mayada likes to place them in small decorative piles.)

6   Place the ghee and garlic in a small pot. Cook on medium-high until the ghee has melted and the garlic just begins to brown, then pour over the fatteh. Sprinkle lightly with cayenne to taste, followed by the toasted pine nuts (if using). Serve immediately or keep warm until serving.

Breaking Fast

Ramadan, the holy month of fasting for Muslims, is a very special period of sharing, socializing, and spending time with family and friends. For Mayada and Ahmad in Syria, it was always spent with their extended families. *Iftar*, the daily evening meal to break the fast, was a celebratory occasion with at least fifteen people around the table and many, many kids running around with glee. Mayada recalls, "We would stay up all night and eat again just before dawn. Then we'd sleep and wake up in the afternoon. And we'd start again! That's Ramadan for you." At the beginning of the month, Ahmad happily pats his stomach and exclaims how skinny he'll become from fasting. Though by the end of the month, with just days until Eid al-Fitr, which marks the end of Ramadan, he jokes that with no eating, no drinking, no cigarettes, Ramadan is no fun at all.

Without being able to eat or even drink a sip of water, cooking for *iftar* relies so much on your other senses and the many times you've likely prepared these dishes before. Here in New Jersey, as she cooks in the hours before *iftar*, without neighborhood mosques playing recitations of the Quran from speakers mounted on their minarets, Mayada makes do with the speaker on her cell phone instead. "When you cook for people who are fasting, they say you will receive extra blessings," she says. With so many dishes to be made, Mayada always worries that they won't be finished in time, but somehow, they always are. Extra hands in the kitchen are always welcome, and non-Muslim friends who can taste the dishes for seasoning are a big advantage—"You always have to have a taster," she says. As each dish is finished, she adds it to the table, covering it with a plate or aluminum foil to keep it warm.

With all the cooking complete, and minutes to spare, the anxious waiting game begins. The boys crowd around a cell phone, counting down the seconds—it's as exciting as when the ball drops in Times Square on New Year's Eve. When the moment of sunset arrives, everyone eats a dried date, as is tradition, and drinks from ice-cold bottles of water. The table becomes momentarily quiet as everyone digs into their first bites of food—except for Jana, who bubbles along as she always does. After dinner, sated and relaxed in the living room, Mayada pulls out *tamar hindi*, a cold, sweet drink of tamarind and lemon to serve alongside the *ma'amoul* or *qatayef*. The night is still young, as *suhoor*, the predawn meal that serves as sustenance for the day, awaits at the other end.

Red Lentil Soup

شوربة العدس

When it's time to cook for *iftar*, the evening meal to break the fast during Ramadan, Mayada turns to a few special-occasion dishes, such as Kibbeh (page 83) and Mehshi Khodar (page 92), in the festive spirit of the holy month. But to round out the table, she often makes this simple, nourishing lentil soup that, like the Fatteh on page 133, is a gentle introduction to solid foods after a long day of fasting. After the traditional dates and a bottle of water (in Mayada's house, it has to be ice-cold, straight out of the refrigerator) are consumed, a few sips of this soup prepare the stomach for the richer dishes to come. Red lentils, which have a softer texture and shorter cooking time than other varieties such as green or black, break down to form a creamy base for the soup. For an even thicker consistency, feel free to use less water.

SERVES 8 TO 10

2 cups dried red lentils

3 quarts water

2 teaspoons ground cumin

Salt

1½ cups parsley, leaves and tender stems, coarsely chopped (about 1 small bunch)

2 tablespoons vegetable oil

2 cloves garlic, coarsely chopped

Juice of 1 lemon

1 Place the lentils and the water in a large pot. Add the cumin and 2 teaspoons salt. Bring to a boil on high, then reduce the heat to medium. Use a spoon to skim away any scum that rises to the top. Simmer gently for about 30 minutes, until the lentils are very soft. Stir in the parsley.

2 Meanwhile, heat the oil in a small pan on medium-high. Add the garlic and cook for 1 to 2 minutes, until it begins to brown. Stir the garlic and oil into the lentils. Stir in the lemon juice. Cook the soup for 15 minutes more, until thickened. Season with salt to taste. Serve immediately.

Stewed White Beans

فاصولياء حب بيضاء مع اللحمه   WHITE FASSOULIA

Though there are two types of *fassoulia* (a version with green beans is on page 41) in Mayada's household, this is one of her favorite recipes, period. White beans are slowly stewed with tomato paste and beef, which along with the bean liquid creates a rich, flavorful broth. It's a special dish for Mayada's family, as they often serve it during big festivals or to break the fast during Ramadan. Serve your *fassoulia* on top of a mound of Rice Pilaf with Vermicelli (page 70).

SERVES 6 TO 8

1 pound dried white kidney beans (2 ½ cups), soaked overnight and drained

¼ cup olive oil

¼ cup vegetable oil

1 ½ pounds stew beef, cut into 1 ½-inch pieces

1 medium onion, thinly sliced (about 1 ½ cups)

One 6-ounce can tomato paste (¾ cup)

2 large cloves garlic, coarsely chopped

Salt and black pepper

1   In a large pot, combine the beans and enough water to cover by 1 inch. Bring to a boil on high. Reduce the heat to medium-low and simmer for 1 hour. Add 1 cup cold water to the beans, return to a simmer, and cook for 30 minutes more, until the beans are tender.

2   While the beans are simmering, heat the olive and vegetable oils in a large pot or Dutch oven over medium-high until very hot but not yet smoking. Carefully add the beef in one layer and cook for 10 to 13 minutes, stirring occasionally, until lightly browned. Add the onions, stir, and cover. Reduce the heat to medium-low and cook for 10 to 15 minutes, until the onions have softened. Add 5 cups water, increase the heat to high, and bring to a boil. Reduce the heat to medium, cover, and simmer for about 30 minutes, until the beef starts to soften.

3   Add the beans and their cooking liquid. Cover and cook for 45 minutes on medium.

4   Add the tomato paste, garlic, 2 teaspoons salt, and 1 teaspoon pepper and stir until thoroughly combined. Cover and cook on medium-low for 25 to 30 minutes, until the beef is very tender. Season with salt and pepper to taste. Remove from the heat and let stand for 10 to 15 minutes to thicken slightly before serving.

الحلويات
Sweets

Sweet Cheese-Filled Pancakes

القطايف   **QATAYEF**

After a long day of fasting, when not even a drop of water is allowed, Mayada's family loves knowing that there are *qatayef* waiting to be devoured after sundown. *Qatayef*, a traditional Ramadan dessert, are small, fluffy pancakes filled with fresh cheese and sometimes nuts, spices, or dried fruit. The half-moon-shaped pastries are fried until golden and crisp, then soaked in a sugar syrup to create a sticky, sweet delight with just a touch of salty tang from the cheese. Though Mayada often makes her own pancakes from scratch, and even the cheese too, ready-made pancakes are widely available during Ramadan at Middle Eastern grocery stores and are an easy, time-saving option.

Note: Mayada uses fresh cheese from her Middle Eastern grocery store, but you can also use grated fresh mozzarella, ricotta, or a combination. A pinch of salt added to the cheese adds a nice contrast to the sweet syrup that saturates the pancakes.

MAKES ABOUT 24 PANCAKES

PANCAKES

2 cups all-purpose flour

1 teaspoon baking powder

½ teaspoon salt

2 ½ cups warm water, plus more if needed

1 teaspoon active dry yeast

Vegetable oil or butter, for greasing the pan

1   Make the pancake batter: In a large bowl, combine the flour, baking powder, salt, water, and yeast. Whisk until smooth and no lumps remain. Cover with a kitchen towel and set in a warm place for 45 minutes to 1 hour, until slightly bubbly.

2   While the batter sits, make the syrup: Place the sugar, water, orange blossom water (if using), and lemon juice in a small pot and stir to combine. Cook on medium-high, stirring occasionally, until the sugar has melted. Remove from the heat and let cool.

3   When the batter is ready, lightly grease a large nonstick skillet with vegetable oil. Heat the pan over medium-high until hot. Give the batter a good stir to recombine. It should have the consistency of pancake batter; if it's too thick, add a little extra water, up to ¼ cup. Working in batches, drop about 2

SUGAR SYRUP

1½ cups sugar

1¼ cups water

1 tablespoon orange blossom water (optional)

1 tablespoon fresh lemon juice

FILLING

1½ cups coarsely grated unsalted mozarella (see Note)

½ cup crème fraîche

Pinch of salt

Vegetable oil, for frying the filled pancakes

tablespoons of the batter into the pan and let it spread to form a 4-inch-wide circle. Cook for 2 to 3 minutes, until the pancakes are just golden brown on the bottom, and bubbly and dry on top; do not flip the pancakes. Transfer to a platter or baking sheet browned side down, and make the remaining pancakes, greasing the skillet again if necessary. Let the pancakes cool completely.

4   Make the filling: In a bowl, stir together the cheese, crème fraîche, and salt.

5   Form the qatayef: Place 2 tablespoons of the filling in the center of a pancake. Fold in half to form a half-moon and pinch the edges to seal well. Repeat with the remaining filling and pancakes.

6   Heat 1 inch of vegetable oil in a deep skillet on medium-high. Working in batches, add the qatayef and cook for 1 to 2 minutes per side, flipping once, until golden brown on both sides. Transfer to a plate lined with paper towels with a slotted spoon to drain and repeat with the remaining qatayef.

7   Transfer the qatayef to a serving platter and drizzle each with 2 to 3 tablespoons of the sugar syrup. Let cool and serve.

Date-Filled Cookies

المعمول   MA'AMOUL

For Mayada, and many other Muslims, these buttery, shortbread-like cookies filled with dates mean Ramadan. When she makes *ma'amoul*, in the generous spirit of the month, she bakes huge quantities at a time. She says it's critical that you have enough to share with all your neighbors and still have some left over for friends and family who will inevitably show up at your door for a welcome social visit. Back in Homs, in one sitting, she would make a batch of *ma'amoul* dough that used more than 25 pounds of flour and 6 pounds of sugar, all painstakingly formed into perfect bite-size cookies with special decorative *ma'amoul* molds.

The dough incorporates *mahlab*, a strongly flavored spice that's commonly used in Middle Eastern and Mediterranean baking. *Mahlab* is made from ground wild cherry pits and has a distinct flavor reminiscent of almond. You should be able to find it, along with *ma'amoul* molds, in a Middle Eastern store or online.

Store any leftover cookies in a sealed container so they retain as much moisture as possible.

SERVES 12 TO 16

1 pound dates, pitted

1 tablespoon unsalted butter, softened

1½ cups plus 1 tablespoon granulated sugar

1 teaspoon active dry yeast

¼ cup warm water

1 cup hot water

6 ¼ cups all-purpose flour

1 teaspoon baking powder

1 teaspoons vanilla powder or 1 tablespoon vanilla extract

1½ teaspoons crushed mahlab

Pinch of salt

1 ¼ cups ghee, melted and cooled

1 In a food processor, process the dates until a smooth paste forms (Mayada uses a meat grinder). Add the butter and process until just combined. Set aside.

2 In a small bowl, combine 1 tablespoon of the granulated sugar and the yeast. Pour in the warm water and let stand for 10 minutes. Combine the hot water and the remaining 1½ cups sugar in a large bowl. Stir until the sugar dissolves. Let cool.

3 In a separate large bowl, combine the flour, baking powder, vanilla, mahlab, and salt. Mix until well combined. Add the ghee and sugar-water. Stir with a wooden spoon (or in a standing mixer) until the dough starts to come together. Use your hands to knead the dough together, folding it and punching down, until combined. Add the dissolved yeast. Use your hands to fold the dough repeatedly, kneading until the dough is

(recipe continues on page 149)

completely combined and smooth. Cover the bowl and set aside.

4   Preheat the oven to 350°F. Roll ¼ cup of dough between your hands. Use your index finger to shape the dough into a cone shape. Place a date filling ball, about ½ inch in diameter, inside. Pinch the hole closed and roll into a smooth ball with no cracks. Press into a 2-inch ma'amoul mold. Release the cookie from the mold and place on a rimmed baking sheet with the pattern up. Repeat with the remaining dough and filling. Place the cookies about 1 inch apart.

5   Bake the ma'amoul for 12 to 15 minutes, until lightly browned at the bottom. Transfer to a serving platter.

VARIATION: SWEET BREAD

Mayada makes a very large quantity of ma'amoul dough and reserves some of it to make unfilled "sweet bread." The dough is rolled out and stamped with decorations before being baked like a large, flat cookie.

On a lightly floured work surface, use a rolling pin to roll disks of dough that are ⅓ inch thick and 5 inches wide. (Alternatively, you can use a bowl as a guide to cut out circles for a more exact shape; knead the scraps together again and roll to make more sweet breads or use for more ma'amoul.) Use a fork and a ma'amoul mold to create a decorative pattern on top. Place on rimmed baking sheets, 1 inch apart. Bake at 400°F for 8 to 10 minutes, until lightly browned on the top.

Rice Pudding with Rose Water, Coconut, and Pistachios

الرز بالحليب

This creamy rice pudding scented with rose water is a big favorite in Mayada's house. "The kids love this pudding so much that whenever I have milk, I have to make it," she says. Depending on your preference, it can be served a number of ways. Served warm, straight out of the pot, the pudding has a thinner consistency and its own comforting appeal. Mayada's kids, though, like it chilled overnight in the fridge so it's very thick, creamy, and cold. No matter how thick or thin you like your pudding, don't forget the last-minute addition of coconut and pistachios.

SERVES 6 TO 8

1 cup short-grain white rice

2 quarts whole milk

2 ½ tablespoons rose water

¾ to 1¼ cups sugar

Sweetened shredded coconut, for serving

Finely chopped unsalted raw pistachios, for serving

1 Place the rice in a medium bowl and add hot water to cover. Let soak for 10 to 15 minutes. Drain the rice, rinse it several times, and drain again.

2 While the rice is soaking, bring the milk to a boil in a large pot on medium-high. (Make sure to keep an eye on it as it gets close to boiling, so it doesn't boil over.)

3 Just as the milk boils, give it a stir, then add the rice and the rose water. Reduce the heat to medium-low and gently simmer for 30 to 35 minutes, uncovered, stirring occasionally, until the rice is softened. Occasionally skim off the skin that forms on top of the milk.

4 Stir in ¾ cup of the sugar; add more if you prefer the pudding sweeter. Increase the heat to medium and cook for 10 to 15 minutes, stirring occasionally, until the sugar is completely dissolved and the rice is fully cooked. Remove from the heat and let cool slightly.

5 Let the pudding cool completely in the pot, then transfer to a bowl or rimmed platter and chill in the refrigerator. (Alternatively, serve warm.) Transfer to serving bowls. Top each bowl with a sprinkle of coconut and pistachios and serve.

Kanafeh

الكنافة

Kanafeh (also called *knafeh*, *konafa*, or *kunafeh*, depending on who's in the kitchen) is another sticky sweet, buttery confection from Mayada's special-occasions repertoire. Although *kanafeh* comes in many different shapes and fillings—flat or rolled up, stuffed with ricotta and mozzarella, spices, or nuts—Mayada builds her beloved Syrian version flat in a pan, using crunchy, golden brown strings of pastry as a bottom and top crust to encase a rich, creamy filling. The pastry—known as kataifi, *kanafeh* dough, or shredded phyllo—is traditionally made by dripping the batter through a perforated tube onto a spinning hot metal surface. The long, thin vermicelli-like strands that form are quickly dried by the hot metal. With lots of ghee and a generous steeping in orange blossom syrup, along with Qatayef (page 142), *kanafeh* is one of Mayada's favorite Ramadan desserts.

SERVES 12

SIMPLE SYRUP

1½ cups sugar

1¼ cups water

1 tablespoon orange blossom water

1 tablespoon fresh lemon juice

PASTRY

1¼ cups ghee

One 1-pound package kataifi, thawed if frozen

2⅓ cups crème fraîche

2 tablespoons sugar

1 cup grated mozzarella (optional)

¼ cup pistachios, coarsely chopped

1　Preheat the oven to 350°F.

2　Make the syrup: Place the sugar, water, orange blossom water, and lemon juice in a small pot and stir to combine. Heat on medium-high, stirring occasionally, until the sugar has melted. Remove from the heat and let cool.

3　Make the pastry: Coat the bottom and sides of a 9-by-13-inch baking dish with ¾ cup of the ghee. Cut the block of kataifi into thick 1½-inch strips. Use your fingertips to loosen three-quarters of the pastry threads or rub them between your hands over the baking dish. Spread the pastry in an even layer in the bottom of the baking dish. Lightly pat down.

4   In a medium bowl, stir together the crème fraîche and 2 tablespoons sugar. Use a spatula or the back of a large spoon to carefully spread the crème fraîche over the pastry, leaving a ½-inch border around the edges. Be careful not to disturb the pastry too much. If you're using it, sprinkle the mozzarella evenly over the cream. Top with the remaining pastry, rubbing it between your hands to separate the threads. Gently pat down. Dot the top of the pastry with the remaining ½ cup ghee.

5   Bake for 45 to 55 minutes, until crisp and golden brown. Immediately drizzle with the syrup. Cut into 3-inch squares, top with the pistachios, and serve.

Chocolate Cookie Bites

كرات شوكولا

This is a recipe that puts Ahmad to work for Mayada. Cookies get crushed and combined with melted butter, chocolate, and milk to create a truffle-like ball that's rolled in shredded coconut. The key is to get the cookies crushed into very fine crumbles—a job that Ahmad patiently did by hand for years, until Mayada found how easy it is to crush the cookies in a plastic freezer bag with a heavy pan during the making of this cookbook; a food processor would make it even easier. This version uses only melted chocolate, but she loves adding Nutella to the mix, too. Mayada admits that these bites may not be originally Syrian, but says plenty of Syrians make a version of them at home. They're in her rotation for celebratory occasions—or she'll sometimes make them for the kids as a special treat.

Note: Mayada uses Goya's Maria cookies, but feel free to use other plain cookies, such as digestive biscuits. You may need to adjust the amount of milk depending on the cookie.

SERVES 8 TO 10

3 packages (3 ½ ounces each) plain cookies, crushed to fine crumbs

1 cup whole milk, plus more if needed

2 tablespoons unsalted butter, melted

1 cup semisweet chocolate chips, melted

2 cups unsweetened shredded coconut

1 In a large bowl, combine the cookie crumbs and milk. Add the butter and chocolate and stir until thoroughly combined. It should be moist enough to mold into balls; if it's too dry, add a little extra milk to reach the desired consistency. Cover the bowl and chill in the refrigerator for 1 to 2 hours, until slightly firm.

2 Spread the coconut on a large plate. Scoop out small portions of the mixture (about 2 tablespoons) and roll between your hands to form 1½-inch balls. Roll the balls in the coconut to coat. Transfer to a serving plate. Serve immediately or keep chilled until serving.

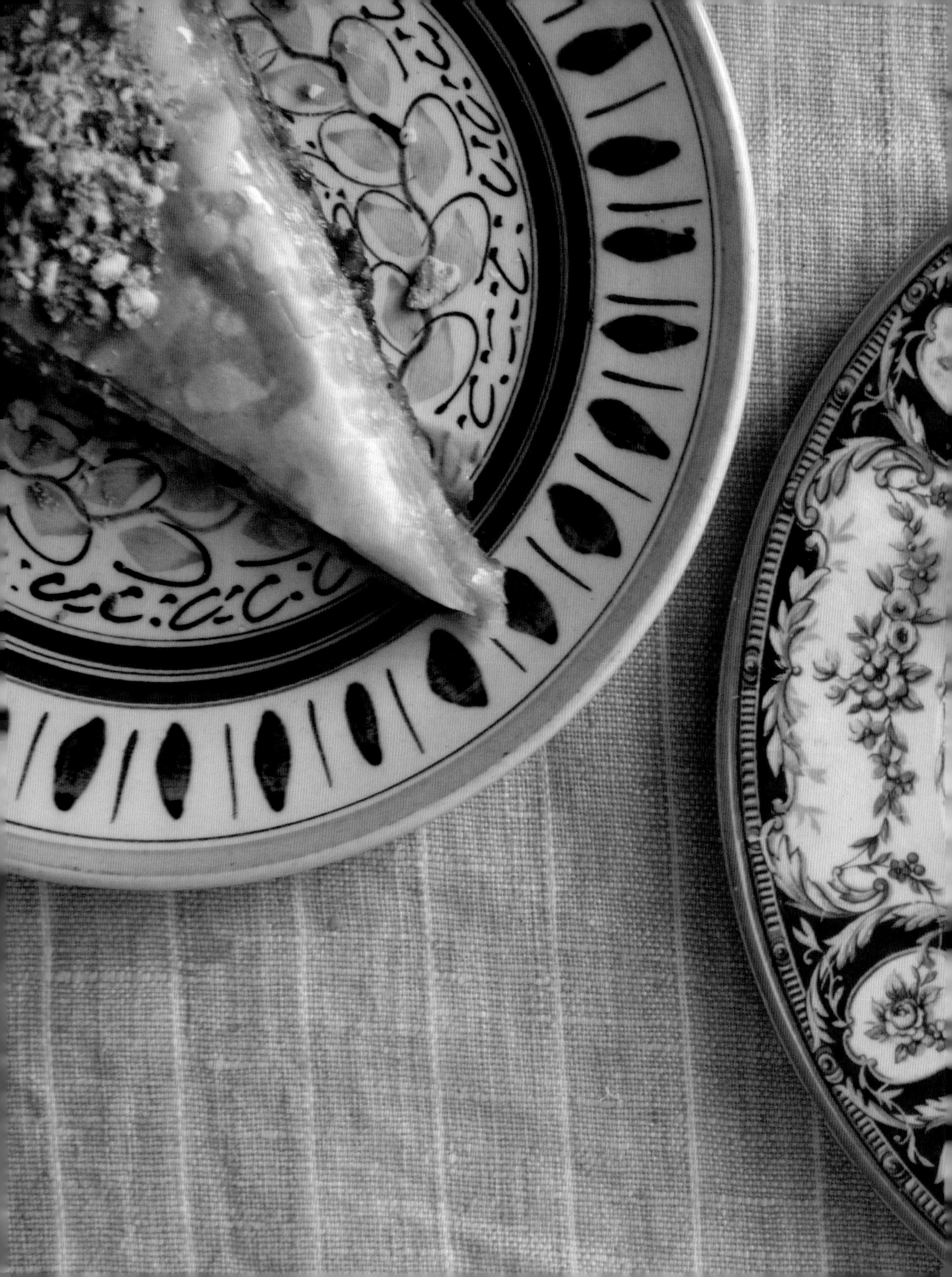

Baklava

بقلاوة

Unabashedly sweet, rich, and buttery, its many layers drenched in orange blossom–scented sugar syrup, Syrian baklava is synonymous with happy occasions in Mayada's life. Although many cultures, from Turkish to Greek, lay claim to this beloved dessert, it is believed that Syrians have been making baklava in some form for almost three millennia—ancient Assyrians layered nuts between thin bread and soaked it in honey syrup. Mayada taught herself to make this dessert, a mainstay at Syrian weddings and neighborhood sweet shops, since arriving in the States so now her family can have a sweet taste of home.

MAKES ONE 8-INCH SQUARE PAN

SIMPLE SYRUP

1½ cups sugar

1¼ cups water

1 tablespoon lemon juice

PASTRY

1½ cups ghee, melted and cooled

½ pound 9-by-14-inch phyllo dough sheets, thawed if frozen

1½ cups finely chopped pistachios, plus 3 tablespoons for garnish

¼ cup sugar

2 tablespoons orange blossom water

1   Make the syrup: Place the sugar, water, and lemon juice in a small pot and stir to combine. Heat on medium-high, stirring occasionally, until the sugar has melted. Remove from the heat and let cool.

2   Preheat the oven to 400°F.

3   Make the pastry: Brush the bottom of an 8-inch square baking pan with 1 tablespoon of the ghee. Lay out the phyllo on a work surface or cutting board. Cut the stack into an 8-inch square, to fit the pan. Keeping the rest of the sheets lightly covered with a damp kitchen towel so they don't dry out, place a square of phyllo in the pan. Coat with 1 tablespoon ghee. Repeat layering phyllo and ghee, ending with ghee, for a total of 10 phyllo layers.

4   In a small bowl, stir together 1½ cups of the pistachios, the sugar, and orange blossom water until well combined. Evenly spread the pistachio filling on top of the phyllo. Top with 10 more alternating layers of phyllo and ghee, ending with ghee.

5 Use a sharp knife or pizza cutter to cut the baklava into triangles: First, cut it into 4 squares by cutting a big plus sign, then cut from corner to corner to make an X; at this point, you'll have 8 triangles. Next, cut from the center of one side of the pan to the center of the adjacent side; continue until you've made 4 cuts and have 16 triangles total. (Alternatively, cut the dough into 16 squares.) Brush the top with the remaining ghee.

6 Bake the baklava for 20 to 30 minutes, until golden and just beginning to brown. Remove from the oven and immediately top with the sugar syrup and the extra pistachios. Let stand until the sugar syrup soaks in and the baklava has cooled, then serve.

Epilogue: How You Can Help Refugees

::⟡⧳⟡::

ANDREW STEHLIK

Senior Pastor, Rutgers Presbyterian Church

In the fall of 2015, members and friends of Rutgers Presbyterian Church began meeting as the Refugee Task Force to plan how the church could help to address the refugee crisis. We agreed to cosponsor a family, and a few months later, four of us were at Newark Airport awaiting the arrival of Mayada and her family. There was a whirlwind of efforts in the few weeks before as we got an apartment ready, furnishing it with items donated by dozens of friends and neighbors. Four hours after the scheduled arrival, three wide-eyed young boys, a sleepy fourteen-month old daughter, and their cautious mother and father emerged: the Abdulhamid family! Six strangers who immediately entered our hearts.

The days and weeks that followed were full of appointments to register benefits, get medical check-ups, and enroll in school, and so many other matters related to a new life in the United States. Someone from our church was with the Abdulhamids every step of the way. It must have seemed confusing, but through it all the children kept Mayada and Ahmad cheerful; waiting in lines for this and that, the sons would tell funny stories and make everyone laugh. This was a family who trusted us and our country with their futures. Leaps of faith for all of us!

The following year, we cosponsored a second family, the Khojas, also from Syria. By then, our network had grown to include other churches and synagogues, and friends and neighbors not affiliated with any faith organization. We found that everyone had their own gifts and talents to share and that there was always plenty to do. We are painfully aware that our efforts are insignificant in light of a refugee crisis so vast. (It's estimated that less than 1 percent of all refugees will be resettled in a new country.) However, we also feel extremely blessed to have the opportunity and resources to help two families create a new reality.

Your purchase of this cookbook will directly assist Mayada and her family, as they receive most of the proceeds from the sales of the book. The remainder will go to the church's Refugee Relief Fund, which provides support to other families and to nongovernmental organizations that help refugees in the United States and overseas.

What more can you do to help?

As a cosponsor, we have partnered with Church World Service, one of nine US nongovernmental organizations that work with the US government to resettle refugees. A list of these organizations can be found in Resources (page 171). Most welcome volunteer help from individuals and groups, and all accept financial donations to assist them in their work. Please contact one of the organizations working in your community and ask how you can help.

The nine resettlement agencies and fifteen other nongovernmental organizations are members of a coalition called the Refugee Council USA. You can visit the council's website and follow them on social media to stay informed and take action about refugee issues in the United States. To learn more about the global crisis and what you can do to help, consult the website of the United Nations Refugee Agency, UNHCR, and the many links found there.

Acknowledgments

MAYADA ANJARI

I want to thank all those who have made this cookbook possible. It was so wonderful to work with Jennifer Sit, to cook with her on weekends and share stories and moments together. I thank her for her passion, good humor, and appetite, and for her talent with both words and food. Thank you to Mira Evnine, who tested the recipes and perfected each dish, and who created the wonderful arrangements that are pictured throughout the book. My food has never looked so delicious! And to Liz Clayman, whose photographs made all the food look so beautiful. It was a pleasure to cook with Mira and Liz during the photoshoot—their style and kindness made sure that everything looks beautiful and gives a sense of family and warmth, just like I hope my cooking does. I'm thankful to Allegra Fisher for her beautiful design of the book, which ties each element of the story together in a wonderful way, and to Elizabeth Gordon for keeping the project running behind the scenes. These special women are impressive in many ways, and you can learn more about the team, including those below, at breadandsaltbetweenus.org.

I extend my deep thanks to Hiroko Kiiffner and Dave Mammen. Hiroko has been an important adviser, and I was thrilled when she offered to publish this book with Lake Isle Press. There is no end to her enthusiasm and kindness. And this project would not have been possible without Dave, who has been there at every step. I thank Dave for his dedication and support, and I know all of us, from my family to the rest of the team, are lucky to know him.

Thanks to Suzanne Fass for her expert copyediting and indexing, and to Dalia El-Newehy, whose help translating between Arabic and English made communication easy and fun. This book would also not be possible without the help of Jeanne Hodesh, Diana Kuan, and Bill Rose at Lake Isle Press. Thank you for your support and help behind the scenes.

My deepest thanks to everyone at Rutgers Presbyterian Church who has helped me and my family, especially Andrew Stehlik, Laura Jervis, and Nancy Muirhead. Thanks also to those at other churches and synagogues who have hosted my fund-raising dinners: Beverly Bartlett at Madison Avenue Presbyterian Church, Brooke Pierce and Nick Zork at Church of the Advent Hope, Mimi Schade and Jeanne Crocker at Unitarian Church of All Souls, and Kathy and Steve Spandorfer at Temple Israel. Many thanks as well to Sima Elali and Bill Bailey, my faithful English teachers.

I'm grateful to Martha Bernabe and Prop Haus, Stacy Adimando and *Saveur* and Test Kitchen, Jonathan Cohen and Delicious Contents, Alina Ramirez and Mud Ceramics, and Meredith Bradford and Staub Cookware. Thank you for your help in testing recipes and for providing beautiful cookware and dishes.

Thank you to Caroline Lang, for contributing her time and know-how to test recipes for the book.

Thank you to Julie Goldstone for the wonderful portraits of me and my family—we will treasure these pictures for years to come. Thanks also to Margarita Garcia Acevedo for her help with the photo shoot, and to Samantha Goldfien for her expert help retouching images.

Thank you to Kathleen O'Keefe of Up Top Acres and Sam Chapple-Sokol for your kindness and help in connecting with José Andrés. And, of course, I'm grateful to José for his time and efforts on behalf of immigrant communities and for his contribution to this book.

And thank you to my family, for their appetites and love.

Everyone involved has volunteered their talents, props, ingredients, and time so that all the proceeds from book sales can help support our family and help other refugees in the United States and overseas. I want to thank them all. And I want to cook for all of them!

JENNIFER SIT

In January 2017, it was the season of Trump: an election night that shocked, an inauguration that numbed, and a refugee ban that infuriated us all. And in that period of demoralizing transition, an unconventional cookbook project was born.

Each person involved with this book—from the publisher, designer, project manager, and copy editor to the photographer, food stylist, and recipe testers—worked on a pro bono basis. To be able to put our seemingly niche skills in the publishing industry to such use was rich payment in itself. Though this book was created in a time of darkness, what it represents is anything but.

Mayada Anjari, it was a privilege and an honor to help bring your story and cooking to the world. I only hope we did them justice. Thank you for your generosity, openness, humor, strength, heart, and trust.

Elizabeth Gordon, without your tireless efforts in managing every wriggling part of this unorthodox process and your eagle-eyed attention to detail, this book wouldn't exist. As a fellow editor and professional wrangler, you have my endless gratitude.

Mira Evnine, your culinary talents and depth of knowledge of Middle Eastern cooking underscore every recipe that graces these pages. Thank you for always going deeper and better with everything you touch.

Liz Clayman, the most delicious foods are not always the prettiest to shoot, and yet, here I am, wanting to dive face-first into every image. Thank you for making this book beautiful to look at.

Allegra Fisher, thank you for giving all of these words, recipes, and images such a handsome home to live in. Liz Trovato, thank you for jumping in when we needed you most.

Hiroko Kiiffner, our publisher, the sense of generosity that envelops this project traces back to you. Thank you for bringing me into this team of amazing women.

 Suzanne Fass, thank you for always being so tough on the page, but such a pleasure in person. (Please don't find a mistake in these acknowledgments.)

Dalia El-Newehy, your easy warmth, graciousness, and hard work on those many Saturdays made this book a joy to work on.

Dave Mammen, whenever I felt that working on this cookbook was tough, I just thought of everything that you and Rutgers Presbyterian Church do and felt humbled and silly. Thanks to you and Rutgers for leading the way with such patience and kindness, and allowing all of us to be part of it.

Rich, watching you work every night and every weekend on the projects that leave your heart happy and brain satisfied makes me want to do more.

Lastly, to you who have found yourself reading this cookbook: I think of the millions of people, including my own parents, who came to this country hoping, believing, dreaming, betting everything on the prospect that America would be better than the place they came from. Let's live up to those dreams and their countless sacrifices. Let's be better.

RESOURCES FOR COOKING

As noted in the Introduction (page 21), the recipes in this cookbook are relatively simple—and most of the ingredients you will need are available in your local grocery store. Middle Eastern groceries will carry specialty items.

In terms of kitchen equipment, falafel scoops are inexpensive, or you can use your hands. You'll need a vegetable corer, to core zucchini and eggplant for Mehshi Khodar (page 92), and you'll want to buy at least one mold to make Ma'amoul (page 146).

A selection of sales outlets is listed here.

Amazon
You can find most ingredients at this online source.
www.amazon.com

Athens Foods
An online source for information about phyllo products, including kataifi (used in Kanafeh, page 154).
www.athensfoods.com

Damascus Bread & Pastry Shop
Syrian flatbread (thinner and wider than the thick pita pockets commonly found in grocery stores) can be purchased at this Syrian bakery in Brooklyn, New York.
195 Atlantic Avenue # 1
Brooklyn, NY 11201
(718) 625-7070
https://places.singleplatform.com/damascus-bread--pastry-shop

Kalustyan's
A vast emporium of spices and specialty ingredients. Shop online or in-store.
123 Lexington Avenue
New York, NY 10016
1 (800) 352-3451
www.foodsofnations.com

Sahadi's
An iconic Middle Eastern grocery in downtown Brooklyn, New York. Shop online or in-store.
187 Atlantic Avenue
Brooklyn, NY 11201
(718) 624-4550
www.sahadis.com

World Spice Market
A modern-day spice bazaar near Seattle's Pike Place Market. Shop online or in-store.
1509 Western Avenue
Seattle, WA 98101
(206) 283-9796
www.worldspice.com

RESOURCES FOR HELPING REFUGEES

Nine nonprofit refugee resettlement agencies provide reception and placement services to refugees under the auspices of the US Department of State's Population, Refugees and Migration Division. The agencies listed below welcome volunteer help from individuals and groups, and all accept financial donations to support their work. Visit their websites for details on the communities in which they work and to learn how to get involved.

Church World Service
Immigration and Refugee Program
475 Riverside Drive, Suite 700
New York, NY 10115
(212) 870-3300; 3042 direct
www.churchworldservice.org

Episcopal Migration Ministries
Domestic & Foreign Missionary Society
815 Second Avenue
New York, NY 10017
(212) 716-6258
www.episcopalchurch.org/emm

Ethiopian Community Development Council
901 South Highland
Arlington, VA 22204
(703) 685-0510
www.ecdcus.org

Hebrew Immigrant Aid Society
333 Seventh Avenue
New York, NY 10001
(212) 967-4100
www.hias.org

International Rescue Committee
122 East 42nd Street
New York, NY 10168
(212) 551-2924
www.theirc.org

Lutheran Immigration & Refugee Service
700 Light Street
Baltimore, MD 21230
(410) 230-2700; 2725 direct
www.lirs.org

US Committee for Refugees and Immigrants
2231 Crystal Drive, Suite 350
Arlington, VA 22202
(703) 310-1130 x3003
www.refugees.org

United States Conference of Catholic Bishops
Migration and Refugee Services
3211 Fourth Street NE
Washington, DC 20017
(202) 541-3000
www.usccb.org/mrs

World Relief
7 East Baltimore Street
Baltimore, MD 21202
(443) 451-1957
www.worldrelief.org

The Refugee Council USA can help you stay
informed and take action about refugee
issues in the United States.

Refugee Council USA
1628 16th Street NW
Washington, DC 20009
(202) 319-2102
http://www.rcusa.org

To learn more about the global crisis and
what you can do to help, consult the website
of the United Nations Refugee Agency,
UNHCR.

UNHCR US office
P.O. Box 20 Grand Central Station
New York, NY 10017
(212) 963-0032
http://www.unhcr.org/en-us

INDEX

A

appetizers. *See* salads and sides; soups; starters and snacks

A'jja, 51

B

Baba Ghanouj, 33

baharat spice mix, 107

Baked Kofta with Pomegranate and Tahini, 60

Baked Kofta with tomatoes, 62

Baked Pasta with Meat Sauce (Ma'ccarona), 44

Baklava, 160

batarsh, 33

Beans, Tomatoes, and Garlic (Green Fassoulia), 41

beef

    Baked Kofta with Pomegranate and Tahini, 60

    Baked Kofta with Tomatoes, 62

    Baked Pasta with Meat Sauce (Ma'ccarona), 44

    Eggplant Stew (Kawaj), 38

    Kibbeh, 83

    Meat Filling for vegetables and grape leaves, 95

    Meat-Stuffed Pies (Meat Fatayer), 128

    Stewed White Beans (White Fassoulia), 139

    Stuffed Grape Leaves (Mehshi Waraq Enab), 102

    Stuffed Vegetables (Mehshi Khodar), 92

    Yogurt Kibbeh, 89

bread

    Cheese Fingers, 131

    Fatayer Dough, 126

    Fatteh with Hummus, 133

    Meat-Stuffed Pies (Meat Fatayer), 128

    Spinach-Stuffed Pies (Spinach Fatayer), 125

    Syrian flatbread, about, 57, 98, 169

    Vegetable and Crispy Pita Salad (Fattoush), 36

    za'atar flatbread, 125

bulgur, about, 65, 75

    Bulgur Pilaf with Vermicelli, 73

    Kibbeh, 83

    Lamb with Bulgur and Rice, 65

    Tabbouleh, 28

    Yogurt Kibbeh, 89

C

Cabbage Salad with Pomegranate Molasses (Malfouf), 32

cheese

    Cheese Fingers, 131

    Kanafeh, 154

    Sweet Cheese-Filled Pancakes (Qatayef), 142

chicken

    Chicken and Potato Soup, 69

    Chicken in the Oven with Potatoes, 78

    Chicken Stew with Jew's Mallow (Mulukhiyah), 116

    Chicken, Vegetables, and Rice (Maqluba), 112

    Kibbeh, 83

    Pan-Seared Coriander Chicken (Shish Tawook), 54

    Spiced Chicken with Rice (Kabsa), 107

    Yogurt Kibbeh, 89

Chocolate Cookie Bites, 157

Cucumber Yogurt, 31

D

Date-Filled Cookies (Ma'amoul), 146

E

Egg Fritters (A'jja), 51

eggplant

    Baba Ghanouj, 33

    Chicken, Vegetables, and Rice (Maqluba), 112

    Eggplant Stew (Kawaj), 38

    Stuffed Vegetables (Mehshi Khodar), 92

Eggs and Tomato (Juz Muz), 48

F

Falafel, 120

Fassoulia, Green, 41

Fassoulia, White, 139

Fatayer

    dough for, 126

    Meat-Stuffed Pies (Meat Fatayer), 128

    Spinach-Stuffed Pies (Spinach Fatayer), 125

Fattoush, 36

G

garlic paste, 31

Grape Leaves, Stuffed (Mehshi Waraq Enab), 102

Green Beans, Tomatoes, and Garlic, Stewed (Green Fassoulia), 41

grilled kibbeh, 88

H

Homs, food of, 25, 33, 36, 54, 57, 65, 78, 83, 88, 92, 146

Hummus, 133

I

iftar, 25, 135, 136. *See also* Ramadan

J

Juz Muz, 48

K

Kabsa, 107

Kabsa Spice, 108

Kanafeh, 154

kataifi, 154

kibbeh, about, 83

    grilled, 88

    Kibbeh, 83

    Yogurt Kibbeh, 89

kofta, about, 60

    Baked Kofta with Pomegranate and Tahini, 60

    Baked Kofta with Tomatoes, 62

L

lamb

    Lamb with Bulgur and Rice, 65

    Lamb-Stuffed Pitas (Marina), 57

    Meat-Stuffed Pies (Meat Fatayer), 128

Lentil Soup, 136

M

Ma'amoul, 146

Ma'ccarona, 44

mahlab, about, 146

    Date-Filled Cookies (Ma'amoul), 146

    Sweet Bread, 149

mains

    Baked Kofta with Pomegranate and Tahini, 60

    Baked Kofta with Tomatoes, 62

    Baked Pasta with Meat Sauce (Ma'ccarona), 44

    Chicken and Potato Soup, 69

    Chicken in the Oven with Potatoes, 78

    Chicken Stew with Jew's Mallow (Mulukhiyah), 116

    Chicken, Vegetables, and Rice (Maqluba), 112

    Egg Fritters (A'jja), 51

    Eggplant Stew (Kawaj), 38

    Falafel, 120

    Fatteh with Hummus, 133

    Kibbeh, 83

    Lamb with Bulgur and Rice, 65

    Lamb-Stuffed Pitas (Marina), 57

    Meat-Stuffed Pies (Meat Fatayer), 128

    Pan-Seared Coriander Chicken (Shish Tawook), 54

    Scrambled Eggs and Tomato (Juz Muz), 48

    Spiced Chicken with Rice (Kabsa), 107

    Spinach-Stuffed Pies (Spinach Fatayer), 125

    Stewed Green Beans, Tomatoes, and Garlic (Green Fassoulia), 41

    Stewed White Beans (White Fassoulia), 139

    Stuffed Grape Leaves (Mehshi Waraq Enab), 102

    Stuffed Vegetables (Mehshi Khodar), 92

    Yogurt Kibbeh, 89

Malfouf, 32

mandi cooking, 107

Maqluba, 112

Marina, 57

Meat Filling for vegetables and grape leaves, 95

meatless dishes. *See also* sweets

    Baba Ghanouj, 33

    Bulgur Pilaf with Vermicelli, 73

    Cabbage Salad with Pomegranate Molasses (Malfouf), 32

    Cucumber Yogurt, 31

    Egg Fritters (A'jja), 51

    Eggplant Stew (Kawaj), 38

    Falafel, 120

    Fatteh with Hummus, 133

    Hummus, 133

    Red Lentil Soup, 136

    Rice Pilaf with Vermicelli, 70

    Sauteed Zucchini Hearts, 99

    Scrambled Eggs and Tomato (Juz Muz), 48

    Spinach-Stuffed Pies (Spinach Fatayer), 125

    Stewed Green Beans, Tomatoes, and Garlic (Green Fassoulia), 41

    Tabbouleh, 28

    Vegetable and Crispy Pita Salad (Fattoush), 36

mehshi, serving, 98

    Stuffed Grape Leaves (Mehshi Waraq Enab), 102

    Stuffed Vegetables (Mehshi Khodar), 92

mezze. *See* salads and sides; starters and snacks

mint, about, 31

Mulukhiyah, 22, 116

P

Pan-Seared Coriander Chicken (Shish Tawook), 54

pasta, about, 44

    Baked Pasta with Meat Sauce (Ma'ccarona), 44

    Bulgur Pilaf with Vermicelli, 73

    Rice Pilaf with Vermicelli, 70

pine nuts, 83, 133

pomegranate molasses

    Baked Kofta with Pomegranate and Tahini, 60

    Cabbage Salad with Pomegranate Molasses (Malfouf), 32

    Lamb-Stuffed Pitas (Marina), 57

    Pomegranate-Tahini Sauce, 60–61

Potato and Chicken Soup, 69

Potatoes and Chicken in the Oven, 78

Q

Qatayef, 142

R

Ramadan, foods for, 25, 57,
    133, 135, 136, 139, 142,
    146, 154
Red Lentil Soup, 136
rice
    Chicken, Vegetables,
    and Rice (Maqluba), 112
    Lamb with Bulgur and
    Rice, 65
    making not sticky, 70
    Rice Pilaf with Vermicelli, 70
    Rice Pudding with
    Rose Water, Coconut,
    and Pistachios, 150
    Spiced Chicken with
    Rice (Kabsa), 107

S

salads and sides
    Bulgur Pilaf with
    Vermicelli, 73
    Cabbage Salad with
    Pomegranate Molasses
    (Malfouf), 32
    Cucumber Yogurt, 31
    Egg Fritters (A'jja), 51
    Eggplant Stew (Kawaj), 38
    Rice Pilaf with Vermicelli, 70
    Sauteed Zucchini
    Hearts, 99
    Stewed Green Beans,
    Tomatoes, and Garlic
    (Green Fassoulia), 41
    Tabbouleh, 28
    Vegetable and Crispy Pita
    Salad (Fattoush), 36
Sauteed Zucchini Hearts, 99
Scrambled Eggs and Tomato
    (Juz Muz), 48
Shish Tawook, 54
soups
    Chicken and Potato
    Soup, 69
    Red Lentil Soup, 136
Spiced Chicken with Rice
    (Kabsa), 107

Spinach-Stuffed Pies
    (Spinach Fatayer), 125
starters and snacks. *See also*
    soups
    Baba Ghanouj, 33
    Cheese Fingers, 131
    Cucumber Yogurt, 31
    Egg Fritters (A'jja), 51
    Falafel, 120
    Fatteh with Hummus, 133
    Hummus, 133
    Lamb-Stuffed Pitas
    (Marina), 57
    Meat-Stuffed Pies
    (Meat Fatayer), 128
    Sauteed Zucchini
    Hearts, 99
    Spinach-Stuffed Pies
    (Spinach Fatayer), 125
Stewed Green Beans,
    Tomatoes, and Garlic
    (Green Fassoulia), 41
Stewed White Beans
    (White Fassoulia), 139
Stuffed Grape Leaves
    (Mehshi Waraq Enab), 102
Stuffed Vegetables (Mehshi
    Khodar), 92
sumac, about, 107
sweets
    Baklava, 160
    Chocolate Cookie Bites,
    157
    Date-Filled Cookies
    (Ma'amoul), 146
    Kanafeh, 154
    Rice Pudding with
    Rose Water, Coconut,
    and Pistachios, 150
    Sweet Bread, 149
    Sweet Cheese-Filled
    Pancakes (Qatayef), 142
Syrian flatbread, about, 57,
    98, 169

T

Tabbouleh, 28
tahini
    Baba Ghanouj, 33
    Baked Kofta with
    Pomegranate and Tahini, 60

Fatteh with Hummus, 133
Pomegranate-Tahini Sauce,
    60–61
Tahini Sauce, 121
Tomato and Scrambled Eggs
    (Juz Muz), 48
Tomatoes, Green Beans, and
    Garlic (Green Fassoulia), 41

V

Vegetable and Crispy Pita Salad
    (Fattoush), 36
Vegetables, Chicken, and
    Rice (Maqluba), 112
vermicelli, about, 70, 73
    Bulgur Pilaf with
    Vermicelli, 73
    Rice Pilaf with Vermicelli, 70

W

White Beans, Stewed
    (White Fassoulia), 139

Y

yogurt
    Baba Ghanouj, 33
    Cucumber Yogurt, 31
    Fatteh with Hummus, 133
    Yogurt Kibbeh, 89

Z

za'atar flatbread, 125
Zucchini Hearts, Sauteed, 99
Zucchini, Stuffed (Mehshi
    Khodar), 92

About the Authors

Mayada Anjari is from Syria. In 2016 she came to the United States from Jordan with her husband and four children under the Refugee Admissions Program of the US government. She is helping her family build a new life by cooking for hundreds of people who have attended her sold out "Dinners with Mayada and Friends" in New York City. She lives in New Jersey.

Jennifer Sit is a cookbook editor and James Beard Award–nominated coauthor of *Senegal: Modern Senegalese Recipes from the Source to the Bowl* with Pierre Thiam. She has edited cookbooks at independent publisher Lake Isle Press and at Blue Apron, including the IACP Award-winning *Blue Apron Cookbook*. She is now a Senior Editor at Clarkson Potter and lives in Brooklyn, New York.